Maynooth College is two hundred years old. Age is honourable and achievement is to be honoured, and both age and achievement will be widely celebrated on the bicentenary. The occasion will see the celebration of Maynooth's original purpose, still continued, the training of priests for Ireland. It will also mark the development of that purpose over two centuries, eventually to include third-level education of men and women in philosophy and theology, in the sciences, and in the arts.

To honour in an appropriate way these two hundred years of teaching, members of the college staff are publishing a series of books in a number of academic disciplines. Edited by members of the College Faculty, these books will range from texts based on standard theology courses to interdisciplinary studies with a theological or religious involvement.

The venture is undertaken with pride in the long Maynooth academic tradition and in modest continuance of it.

YOU ARE MINE

Myles Rearden, CM

You Are Mine

A VIEW OF THE SPIRITUAL LIFE

Do not be afraid,
For I have redeemed you;
I have called you by your name,
You are mine.
Isaiah 43:1

the columba press

First published in 1994 by
the columba press
93 The Rise, Mount Merrion, Blackrock, Co Dublin

Designed by Bill Bolger
Origination by The Columba Press
Printed in Ireland by
Colour Books, Dublin

ISBN 1 85607 105 7

Acknowledgements

HarperCollins Publishers Ltd for permission to quote from the Grail translation of the Psalms and from Betty I Knott's translation of *The Imitation of Christ*. Darton, Longman and Todd for permission to quote from Jean Vanier, *Community and Growth*, and Karl Rahner, *Theological Investigations, Vol 6*. The Crossing Press, Freedom, California for permission to use material from *12 Steps to Freedom* by Kathleen W. Faber and Faber for permission to quote from T. S. Eliot, *Four Quartets*. Alba House, New York for permission to quote from Francois Jamart, *Complete Spiritual Doctrine of St Thérèse of Lisieux*. Dominican Publications, Dublin for permission to quote from Austin Flannery (ed), *The Conciliar and Post-Conciliar Documents*. The Institute of Carmelite Studies, Washington DC for permission to quote from *The Collected Works of St John of the Cross* translated by Kieran Kavanaugh and Otilio Rodriguez. The State University of New York, Albany, NY, for permission to quote from *The Path to No-Self* by Bernadette Roberts. All quotations from the bible are from *The New Jerusalem Bible*, published and copyright 1985 by Darton, Longman and Todd and Doubleday & Co Inc, and used by permission of the publishers.

Contents

Introduction

My aim in this book is to express how I experience spirituality and understand it. It is a personal book. But since I am a priest, my experience and understanding of spirituality have been worked out in close partnership with other people, especially those I have ministered to, and in particular, over the last five years, seminarians of St Patrick's College, Maynooth. Together we have learned a good deal about God and about people. It is to them that I dedicate the book.

I like Pope Paul VI's statement that people want witnesses more than they want teachers, and only teachers who are also witnesses.[1] So in this book I have taken the conscious risk of putting my experience of life on public view. I am encouraged by the fact that when I have found other people doing that, it has often been very convincing.

I am also putting forward a certain tradition of spirituality, a particular approach to living the gospel. It is the Vincentian tradition, in which I, like my father and grandfather before me, have lived. Because that is the tradition which for more than a hundred years the spiritual directors at Maynooth College have handed on, it seems right to address spirituality from that viewpoint in a work associated with the bicentary of the foundation of the College. Indeed, the Irish Vincentians were founded from (though not by) Maynooth.

By way of setting down markers to show where I stand, I should say that there are two recent statements about spirituality that I cannot accept. One is found in Karl Rahner's essay, 'Theology of Freedom', and goes like this:

> The original relationship to God is love of neighbour. If man becomes himself only by the exercise of love towards God, and must achieve this self-mastery by a categorial action, then it holds good that the act of love of neighbour is the only categorial and original act in which man attains the whole of the concretely given reality, and finds the transcendental and supernatural, directly experienced experience of God.[2]

7

If God is not identical with our neighbour, and can be known not to be identical with our neighbour, then people can love God in God's self. People's actual experience of God in their own selves and in nature must be honoured, as well as their experiences of God in others, for example, in the poor. What Rahner says in this influential sentence seems to me to make for a one-dimensional spirituality which is not very inspiring. Much else that he writes I have found extremely inspiring.

The other recent statement I cannot accept is quite similar:

> I believe that grace operates first and foremost in and through our transcendental desire to know other people and, through them, to get in touch with the mystery of God. I also suspect that the choice to go beyond egocentric concerns in this way, by focusing attention on the inner experience of another person, is not only the primordial act of will, it is arguably the pre-requisite for all other derivative acts of decision making.[3]

It comes from a book by a confrere of mine, Fr Pat Collins, whose work I admire. The reason I cannot accept this particular statement (which he makes extremely tentatively) is that experience, both my own and others', leads me to the view that grace operates in many different ways. These include personal relationships, but not necessarily in first place. How many of the conversion experiences of the saints had much to do with the desire to get to know other people? I think religious experience has to be allowed to happen as it happens, and not forced into a mould.

Accordingly, in this book I try to explore all the dimensions of spiritual living, while giving it some clarity of focus by presenting a particular spiritual tradition. I present spiritual living as a growth process, and an arduous one at that; or a journey like the one on which Abraham set out when he heard the call, 'Leave your country, your kindred and your father's house for a country which I shall show you.'[4] I hope that the book will encourage people to set out on this journey, and come to experience loving union with God.

There are numerous people who have been of great assistance to me in writing *You Are Mine*. Among them are my colleagues in the ministry of spiritual direction here at Maynooth, Fathers Jim Rafferty and Sean Hanafin; other colleagues in spiritual direction, Sisters Rosemary Alexander and Mary Toner, and Fathers Mark Noonan and Richard McCullen; Ms Lucille McDonald, Brother Frank Sherlock, Father Jimmy Doherty of Derry Diocese, and

Father Andrew Spelman. They have all read drafts of the book, or of parts of it, and helped me with their comments, sometimes quite trenchant ones. I am very grateful to them all.

Finally, the Structure of *You Are Mine* is as follows. The two middle chapters, four and five, are the most important because they contain an account of how people grow spiritually during their lives. The three chapters that precede them anchor spiritual growth in the experience of individual people, of the church, and of various cultural groups. Of the last three chapters, six deals with ways to grow spiritually, seven deals with spiritual growth that begins with a condition of addiction, and eight deals with the completion of spiritual growth in and after a person's death.

Myles Rearden, CM
St Patrick's College,
Maynooth.
Easter Sunday
April 3rd 1994

Notes:
1. *Evangelii Nuntiandi,* Vatican Polyglot Press, 1975, p52, n 41.
2. *Theological Investigations*, vol 6, DLT, London 1969, p 189f.
3. *Intimacy and the Hungers of the Heart*, Columba Press, Dublin 1991, p 129.
4. Genesis 12:1.

CHAPTER ONE

Living Spiritually

What else have I in heaven but you,
Apart from you I want nothing on earth.
Psalm 72

Seeking God

By spiritual living, I mean a person's movement towards union with God. It is my deepest personal conviction that this movement towards union with God is the central reality in anyone's life. I say this very much aware of how different people are from each other. A large part of this chapter tries to show just how great the difference is. Yet everyone finds his or her place within the common human longing and seeking for God. And that is only a pale reflection of God's seeking and longing for us.

How can I or anyone be as certain of that as I am? Did people tell it to me, when I was young and impressionable? Yes, many people did. They continue to do so, though I am no longer young or impressionable. Do I find it proved by rational or scientific arguments? Certainly. I know enough philosophy and theology to be intellectually certain that a person's central living movement is towards union with God. But someone's deepest personal certainty is more than intellectual. My personal certainty is based on everything in my outer life and in my inner life. Everything I have been able to learn by study and experience comes together in the longing and searching for union with God. I mean, a God who loves me, and whom I am able to love.

None of us resemble each other enough to be able to say: 'This is how I know about the centrality in human life of the movement towards God, so it is how you will know it too.' My personal certainty is an assertion of what it is to be myself. Why would other people share my certainty? Because they also can only define themselves in terms of their movement towards God. Defining themselves thus involves a leap of faith. To acknowledge that God holds that place in one's self-definition does not strictly follow from any evidence. It is something individual people know from experience, and something confirmed by faith.

So you and I need not agree about God's place in our lives. Or, if we do, our agreement need not constitute the most important bond between us. Both these things involve more pushing forward in faith. To live is to push forward like that – into friendship, into a way of life, into work, taking sometimes wise and sometimes foolish risks. Risk cannot be avoided if we are to be alive at all. But I would stand to lose too much if I risked living for anything less than God. Having fun, becoming famous, being strong financially, are all things worth aiming at. But neither separately nor together can they bring out the whole of what it is to be a human being. Only God, only moving towards God, does that. And this, together with the fact that God is moving towards us, is what produces spirituality. What exactly spirituality is for me, I will try to express later in the book. But first I want to say something about what and who God is for me, what and who I think we human beings are like, and what resources a human person has for going in search of God.

Knowing God: Father

God, as I know him, is the maker of the world, of everything, myself included. And he is the Father of Jesus of Nazareth, who is himself God. And again, God speaks to me and is present in the depths of my mind and heart, though he does not always make his presence felt there. This is a way of seeing God as Trinity. Since I am writing spirituality and not theology, I do not wish to consider whether this knowledge of mine corresponds fully with the Christian doctrine of the Trinity, though some theologians have told me that it does. What I am sure of is that God is Creator, Saviour and indwelling Spirit, and that I can know him. I know that I can try to live for him. I also know that I can ignore him and his claims on me. That is what I know personally about God. I will expand it now in connection with each of the three ways I know God.

   That there must be a God, if there is to be anything rather than nothing, seems to me to be true. What the God who made the world is like is a question that leads into a fascinating scientific question: What is the world really like? We do not know the answer to that. But there are exceptional moments when the world reveals its power, beauty, and remoteness. At times like that, it forbids me to take it for granted And it is then that I find the world speaking to me about God. Looking across a harbour with its islands and the land, the town, the hills on the other side, under an indescribable sky. Getting the sense of life in a city with its millions of inhabitants. Being with an individual person when he or she is most alive and present. These are experiences that give me some sense of the greatness of God. They are not experiences that absorb me into the world. They are experiences that leave me somewhat disengaged from the world. I also get some sense of God's greatness on the occasions when I have got an inkling of what great scientists and philosophers were saying about the world; again I am disengaged, seeing things through their eyes. This ability to stand back from the world makes it possible to sense God as very gentle. It helps me to sense that for all the power of the world and its God, he does not want it to extinguish me. These experiences, when they come, let me see God both as immense and very, very kind. In such experiences, there is nothing for it except to honour God and offer myself to him. I can avoid the experience, though, if I want to. I can break it off, by not making the effort necessary to keep it up.

Knowing God: Son

From my earliest years, I have been brought up in the Christian religion, in the Catholic Church. I have learned that the very God who created everything has a Son who is God like himself, but who is also a human being. God's Son is a man, because he took human nature in the womb of a Jewish girl named Mary. I learned these things with the immediacy of present fact. My people celebrated the day of the birth of Jesus, God-made-man, even more joyfully than that of any member of my family. He was physically present to me in the sacrament of the eucharist. As time went on and I was initiated into other sacraments, like confirmation and penance, I got to appreciate the reality of this presence more and more. The character of Jesus became clearer to me as I learned something of the scriptures that tell what is known of his life, and say what that life signifies. Jesus Christ appeared so powerfully attractive to me that I had no difficulty in agreeing to devote my life entirely to him, when it began to seem that this was what he was asking of me. I was ultimately delighted when I was ordained a priest. The long years of testing and enquiry and training convinced me, and everyone else involved, that God really was calling me. What I have learned from life lived in that service is that there is no limit to the astonishing power of Jesus and his teaching. I have also learned that there is not much limit either to my capacity for misunderstanding the teaching of Jesus and responding to it in quite unacceptable ways. As in the case of knowing the Creator, it is the exceptional times that make everything come just right. Only, with Jesus, in these times I am not at a distance, but completely involved in what is happening. And there is progress, a definite sense of growth in union with Jesus.

There is also, again as in the case of the Creator, the clear realisation that I could marginalise Christ. I could concentrate on
someone or something else. I could set up some other goal instead
of accomplishing his work. I could do that even while pretending
to do his work. The involvement with Jesus, however close it gets,
or has yet got, is not such as to imprison me. My sins, and what
appear to be the sins and betrayals of others, have one advantage.
They make it clear that in remaining faithful to Jesus Christ I do
not cease to be a free person. Indeed, what experience has taught
me to date is that it is not fidelity to Christ, but unfaithfulness to
him, that imprisons me.

Knowing God: Spirit
The presence of God to my inner self is difficult to write about. He
seems to speak to me and to attract me from inside myself. But it
is very hard to express. That may be because I very often like to
distance myself as much as possible from my inner life. I can ignore
it. I can speak about it whether to myself or others in vague or life-
less words. I can try to satisfy myself with unexpressed feelings.
Things like shame at doing something wrong, or delight at meeting someone good, are often felt. But they are often, half-delib-
erately, no more than felt. And they slip away, instead of being
kept as stages of interior growth. It is only in recent years that I
have begun to appreciate the reality of God within me. I have
come into contact with people who were very attentive to expressing their inner sense of God. I have taken up getting spiritual
direction again. That makes me recognise how I feel about God.
Even more, since starting to give spiritual direction, I have seen
how God speaks and works in other people. I know many people
who have been attending to God within them since their teens. As
a result they have become and are becoming very holy. They also
have to suffer a lot, more in their inner lives than in their outer
lives. The 'dark nights' and 'purifications' that saints have written
about are everyday experiences for hundreds of people I know.

Trinity
Although it may seem a big thing for me to say, I feel that one of
the greatest benefits that the Christian religion has bestowed on
the world is the assurance that there is only one God. And that in
God there are three persons, the Father, whose life consists in giving life to the Son, and the Spirit, who is the union of the Father
and the Son loving each other. This fact enables us to see that the
Creator, and Jesus Christ, and the Spirit within us, are only one

God. As we experience them, the three avenues of approach to God correct and balance and stimulate each other. They give us a knowledge and a sense of the presence of God. They enable us to live for God in every area of human life. And the God we meet in these three ways leaves us with the awful power of rejecting him.

Six Lives
When St Francis de Sales long ago wanted to emphasise that spirituality is for everyone, he did so by mentioning different trades and professions. I think that to make the same point today, we need to mention different individuals in their different life situations. So I want to try to summon up six people, three men and three women, of different ages and different situations in life, not in order to draw any conclusion about what any of them should do, but simply to remind myself and my readers of the real world where spirituality has to be lived. Everything in this book applies in one way or another to Ken and Sinéad, to John and Lily, to Michael and Edith. The six of them are not going to reappear very often in this book, but they are going to be in the background all the time. These characters stand for the potential readers of the book, or at least, the people to whom what it says applies. In creating these characters, I have two aims. First, for them to be credible. Second, for their lives to take a positive direction, at least in the end. This is because spirituality is about salvation, and salvation is about ending well. What that means is that none of the six exemplifies the ultimate tragedy of not being saved, so that at this stage of the book we do not have that awful possibility too much before our minds. I admit that, as a result, the present selection of characters to stand for us may seem unduly bland.

Ken
Ken left school after his Junior Certificate. He is still too young to get the dole. Coming up to Christmas, he got a job helping to clear up a bar at night, but mostly he has nothing doing. When he gets a bit of money, he likes a game of snooker. He can't go out with girls much because they don't want to go around with someone who has nothing. He likes to go around with other fellows like himself, because they are not too hard with each other and they help each other out. God seems very far away: He doesn't help much. Some of Ken's friends go to Mass an odd time, most never. When Ken goes to Mass, say for a funeral, he feels out of things, not involved. When he felt very lonely once he started to pray, and after a while he felt all right. But the odd time is enough for

that. What he'd like would be for a big man he could respect to come along and offer to take him on for something – he'd travel anywhere to meet a man like that, England, Australia, anywhere. But as for now, at least he gets something to eat at home and his clothes washed. So Ken is waiting for something to turn up.

What can happen to Ken, spiritually? He could be picked up by someone who takes an interest in him, maybe puts him in the way of a job, some religious organisation probably, most likely one of the sects. In theory, he could set out in an individualistic sort of way, or with some friends, to implore God to help him, but in practice that is hardly likely. He could fall in with some criminal or near-criminal group, and after feeling guilty about it for a while, forget all thought of God. For example, he might get into the drug scene. He might talk to his mother or his father or some other person about what is happening and see what they would advise. But the chances are that he will be left to his own devices and not see much hope in God.

Ken is basically crying out for a miracle. Unless one comes, he depends on an approach by someone in the secure adult world who can make him a decent offer with some prospects, with God and the things of God as part of the offer. He wants to be brought into some social group where he will be valued and challenged. He knows instinctively that he is worth that, and he is on the watch for it.

Sinéad

Sinéad left school two years ago and considers herself very lucky to have got a receptionist's job at a big camera repair workshop. She doesn't know it, but the manager considers himself lucky too at getting her for the job; she has a way of making everyone feel welcome and of calming down even the most troublesome cus-tomers, just by being herself. At home she is the same. Her father has been off work since a back injury years ago, and when he gets depressed, he has only to think of Sinéad and he feels his life hasn't been a complete failure. His only wish is that when she gets married she will get a husband who deserves her.

Sinéad knows some of her strengths. She knows that people like her, and that she can get the best out of them, and she does not often make mistakes. She appreciates her faith and goes to Mass, but no one considers her very religious, not a charismatic or anything like that. She likes boys, especially some of the ones at work, but she is in no hurry to get involved with any of them.

Most of her affections are still taken up with her parents and her younger brothers and sisters at home.

One of her aunts, who saw a sister of her own let life pass her by while she looked after her ageing mother, gave Sinéad a hint last Christmas to be thinking about her future. It made Sinéad feel uncomfortable, but she knows her aunt is right – it's like a call from another wider world where she belongs. She has made an appointment to meet one of her former teachers after work one day next week to see what she recommends by way of improving her promotion prospects in the job and widening her personal contacts in life. She even prayed about it a bit at Mass last Sunday, though apart from asking for help like that, it never crossed her mind to go to God, as it were, for advice. There is no level of adult religion available to Sinéad. Sometimes she hears a priest or a nun on the radio who sound as if they are coming from somewhere deep and holy, and sometimes she gets the same feeling when she listens to a reader or a preacher in the church, but those moments are gone almost as soon as she realises they are there. A really great person, but somewhat isolated, that's Sinéad.

What eventually happens is that Sinéad falls in love with one of the lads from work and, in due course, they get married and settle down to have children. In the meantime, she did a typing and computer course and she takes in some work at home. It was when the children started primary school that Sinéad linked up with her wider world. She became involved with other parents and the teachers, and her skills at personal relations really proved valuable. Helping to prepare the children for first communion, and discussing things that came up with the teachers, enabled her to become articulate regarding her faith, and she started to get very interested in it, especially as some very worthwhile talks and even a weekend retreat were organised by the parish. At thirty-five, Sinéad found a new life opening up in front of her.

John

There are times when John wakes up in the morning and feels over again the pain that his wife is gone. He doesn't feel anything about the young doctor she slipped away to Australia with, he just misses her. And he feels for the young ones too, growing up without their mother. But the work of two hundred acres doesn't leave him much time to think about it during the day – something to be thankful for. And now that he is getting involved in local politics, it is something to fill the evenings. Not that the pain of it ever goes away completely. Pity she wasn't there for the second youngest's first communion last week, or the medal the oldest lad brought back from the sports.

John does not know what to make of Sunday Mass. He keeps it up, even though there are plenty around who are finding more excuses than usual to miss it. Times it seems real, a real touch of God, other times he feels resentment at the way the wifeless and childless priest stands up there talking about things that are worlds away from John. But with all that, the land on a dewy morning has a touch of God about it, and a cow dropping a calf is the kicking of new life. If farming was only animals and crops, John could be a saint. But it's the money that ruins it: headage subsidies, bank repayments, insurance schemes, tax returns, the price of cattle – not much chance of being a saint with that lot, and if God backs up the law, maybe not much chance of heaven either.

John grew strong playing nature at her own game, forcing the land to give him and his a satisfying living. His God meets him coming down many roads, but he's not too sure if is the same God giving nature its power, and the law its authority, and putting the question marks in the children's eyes. What he wants is a God who can feel his satisfied tiredness and his untameable pain and his hope and his despair. What he wants is a God whose commandments do not crush him and whose mysteries do not make the world even harder to make sense of. What he wants is a priest who can stand shoulder to shoulder with him, looking into the eyes of this crazy life. And to tell the truth, he would not mind bringing another woman into his own and the children's life, or at least finding someone who can tell him why not, and sound as if he or she knows.

John needs the companionship of men and women of his own age and character, who can suffer and who can turn suffering round into something like satisfaction and even contentment. If he's going to meet Christ he must be able to know that Christ knows what's happening. For his personal life he has not much need of a book-learned priest or preacher. The only part of his life where he could see a bit of that fitting in is the politics. He has enough economics and accounting to see what is going on, but it is more than the wisest man in Ireland can say which of it is wrong and which is right, or if those words still have any meaning. People who make religion their trade have a job on hand when they try to be honest with John.

Lily
Lily frightens some people, though she has an excellent manner

with the customers in the shop, is fiercely devoted to her three children, and tolerant of her easy-going husband, Ray. He drives a milk tanker for one of the big dairy firms, and she is fighting a successful battle against a supermarket chain to keep the family general store going. People said she hadn't a chance when the big firm moved into the other end of town five years ago, but her brilliant head for business, plus her manner and local knowledge, plus her ability to have in stock exactly what there was a demand for, made her a winner.

Being abused systematically between the ages of five and ten did not destroy her, but it gave her a powerful will to get from the world exactly what she wanted. And now she has it: an undemanding marriage, two boys and a girl between eleven and fifteen, and, best of all, a fight on her hands. On her first communion day she decided that God had no right to expect anything from her, and soon after her confirmation she decided that God, for all practical purposes, did not exist. For the sake of the children, and for the sake of business, she kept on the mask of religion, but her real religion is imposing her will on life. She laughs sometimes when her mother calls her Tiger Lily, but she knows it is true.

Sunday evenings in the summer are her worst time. The children are out playing with their friends, Ray is usually away by four on a collection run, not many people like to drop by for a chat, and Lily is left for the only time of the week with nothing to do. Nothing except a black rage. It takes her body over with such intensity that she does not know whether to call it hot or cold. Once she thought of taking up a suggestion she read in a digest and getting some paper and paints to express her mood. But that felt like weakness, so she just lives it through, the hours before the children get in for their tea and have to be organised for school next day. Sometimes through the window she sees old nuns out for a walk, all smiles and quiet talk, and she wonders if she is in the same world as them.

It hasn't happened yet, but what is eventually going to open things up for Lily is an invitation from a local charitable society for her to visit two old women living alone, on a Sunday evening. She decides to give it a try, as an escape from her mood more than anything else. One of them can hardly move at all, but she is very alert and a great listener. Lily finds herself beginning to talk about herself for the first time in her life, and in the end tells the old woman everything that happened to her when she was growing up. The old woman did not say anything about God, in fact she said very little about anything, but gradually Lily found her fierceness going and even began to think affectionately about God sometimes. She began to feel that going to Mass was not like wearing a mask any more. One thing though, she did not lose her business touch, and the supermarket chain decided against moving into her end of the town.

Michael

Michael looks at his diary for the day: a funeral in the morning, a young woman killed in a hit and run accident, leaving three children and a husband working in England; a meeting of the school management board at 2.30, and a meeting of the diocesan finance council at 4.00, two couples to be met about marriages in the evening. Pity he couldn't get one of the curates to take on one of them, but their diaries are likely full too. Sometimes he wishes that the rumours putting him forward for auxiliary bishop had proved true, though the higher profile wouldn't really suit him: anyway, whenever he meets the auxiliary bishop at the finance council, it is obvious that the man is run off his feet. Isn't there a story by Chekov about the life of a subordinate bishop of some kind in the Russian Orthodox Church ...? Maybe he'd get a bit of reading done tonight, give the news and that wretched news analysis programme a miss and pick up something that takes a broader and deeper view of life for a change. Shouldn't he have taken the chance of going to UCC forty years ago – he might be a professor now, like the fellow who sat beside him at school: likely he'll be interviewed on the news analysis programme. No, by God, he has some chance of saving his soul where he is, instead of trying to swim around in the murky world of politics, especially academic politics. At least, today's diary is keeping him in touch with the realities of life – and death, God help us. How's that poor devil working on the sites in England (if he hasn't been laid off) going to manage the three kids? You'd have to admire anyone setting out into marriage these days. That's another thing he'd missed – a wife and family. In fact the worst of both worlds – a friendship with someone else's wife twenty years ago had done more to finish his chances of being auxiliary bishop than the qualifications of the man who got it. For sure, the hand of God works in strange ways. Never thought while listening to talks on Providence in the seminary that the hand of God would sink to moving quite like that. She's lady captain of the golf club this year, isn't she – must give her a ring to kid her about that. Anyway, there's just time to say a bit of the office and even do a bit of praying before he has to get over and see that the church is ready for the funeral, and then back to write out a special paragraph for the tragic death homily. Hopes to God the Holy Spirit is there to touch someone with what he says.

Michael has been working and living for God all his life, and is certain that living that kind of life now is as confused and stressful as in the immediate aftermath of the crucifixion. The combination of faith and knowing that his job is vital and that he is good at it keeps him going, that and the spirit of the diocesan priests. But he would like to feel closer to God, to understand young people better, and to see more clearly what is needed for the church and for the parish.

Edith

Edith was one of the first women in the country to get a degree in electrical engineering, and for some years now she has been the brains of a major electronics company's research and development unit. Her husband is a senior partner in an accountancy firm, and they have succeeded in giving each other the freedom to pursue their separate careers, as well as in bringing up their five children, four boys and a girl. At school, Edith not only developed her flair for mathematics enough to win through in what was virtually an all-male world, but also acquired a life-long respect and love for her faith. She has rarely missed daily Mass since the children learned to cook their own breakfast (Ned, her husband, learned that on their honeymoon), and she keeps herself informed about what is going on in the church (she is a Catholic, Ned is not), in academic life, and in the country at large. She made it her business early on to seek out some leading Catholic thinkers in the country who would discuss things honestly with her, and has recently found a nun to be her spiritual director.

It was just as well that Edith found someone who could be a director for her, because disillusionment with the church and with society in general had begun to get a grip on her. She was getting tired of the number of clerics who felt they had either to patronise her or to avoid her, she missed the dignity of the Latin liturgy she had been brought up on, and thought the parish priest had been ill-advised to entrust the readings at Mass to young people in their early teens. Too many standards were dropping and values disintegrating for her to avoid feeling some bitterness; though she was grateful that most of the hypocrisy of former times was also gone. It was Sister Dorothy, her spiritual director, who helped her to notice the rising tide of her bitterness, and more important, to realise that inner peace could grow from God alone, rather than from human groups or individuals or institutions. Edith met Dorothy at a weekend retreat, and soon after began going to her monthly for spiritual direction. Not that Dorothy was very directive, but she did help Edith to become aware of herself having a very close relationship with Christ, and of not being as dependent on family or church as she thought she was, and of being able to appreciate them all the better for seeing them in the light of her relationship with Christ.

Edith is beginning now, with her family reared, to discover the reality of God's care for her, and of her capacity for caring for others. She is planning to begin something practical in this line, and is investigating whether she could do best by joining a support-group for married couples (Ned is interested in that too), or getting a word-processor and making something of a career for herself in writing, or just re-activating her old friendships and forming new ones. She is also planning a prayer-life for herself, including quite a long period of contemplative prayer each day. And she is beginning to discover the value of fairly frequent confession, which she had dropped quite a long time ago. Altogether she is feeling quite excited about how things are going, and feels almost as if her life was entering a second spring.

Responding to God

Spirituality, for those six people and for everyone, is movement towards God, towards union with God. It is responding to what a person knows and feels of God. It is entirely personal, as individual as each of the individual lives I have just conjured up out of experience. Spirituality is uniquely rich in every person's case. That is because God is big enough to be fully present for everyone. But spirituality is also communal, as people are. It is not just something private. So people can speak to one another and write for one another about who and what God is for them. Fundamentally that is what the church is. It is the assembly of people who share with each other their experience of God, and move together towards union with God. There are three levels of experience at which everyone can progress towards God: knowledge, feeling and will.

Knowledge of God

Knowledge itself is the first step towards union with God. A person begins to move towards God when he or she, just as himself or herself, knows something of God. That is faith. Faith may come in all the dignity of ago-old culture and religion. It may come with the shock of new discovery. It may come with something of both. But at root, faith is going completely beyond this world. Faith is the glimpsed reality of God. A glimpse of the reality of God is not something any person can achieve for himself. Faith, everyone's faith, is a gift from God. (Though it is possible to know that there is a God by personal reflection.) Faith grows out of the initiative God takes in communicating himself to a person, every person, separately and together. Helping someone to stay with, and to develop his or her sense of God, is the greatest service anyone can do for someone else.

Being attracted to God

People do not live on the level of knowledge alone. So the movement towards God is not by knowledge alone, though it may begin there. Human beings also live on the level of their feelings and their wills. Growing towards God takes place on these levels also. Allowing our deepest feelings to unfold themselves in relation to God is a very important stage in approaching him. This is not quite the same as saying that spirituality is essentially emotional. It is a difficult question whether the feelings proper to spirituality are emotions. Perhaps we should keep the word 'emotion' for feelings between human beings, and not between us and God. It is an important part of spirituality not to forget that God is God, far beyond us. Emotions may be more of an obstacle to movement towards God than a help, if they block our really spiritual feelings. But there must be some real feeling in spirituality.

Choosing God

Choice of God, commitment to him, resoluteness, being steady and patient, are all things we associate with the will. They are also part of spirituality. Will-acts like these can happen without any knowledge or feeling. Aren't there people whose religion is pure duty? But a movement towards God, which tries to go by will alone, loses its momentum. Only as God communicates himself to the mind and to the feelings can God be lastingly responded to by the will. A really supernatural opening of the mind and of the feelings lies at the root of spirituality. Still, a fully grown spirituality depends on what a person, or a group, or a whole society, is prepared to do and to suffer for the love of God. In other words, it depends on the human will.

CHAPTER TWO

Spiritualities

O where can I go from your spirit,
or where can I flee from your face?
Psalm 138

Introduction

'Each person's spirituality is unique and particular.'[1] There are, fundamentally, as many spiritualities as there are people. I would say that there are even more. Our freedom means that it is up to ourselves not only to find our way in life, but to choose our way from a range of possible ways. The same applies at the social level. There are many ways for a society to be itself, whether it is a small society like a newly married couple, or a nation or even the whole world. I think that the pluralism that people insist on so much today stems, not only from our experienced need to discover who we really are, but also from on our need to decide how to be who we really are. I am convinced that nobody should oppose that kind of pluralism, especially anyone whose religion comes from Jesus Christ. Jesus is a person who recognised himself as Son of God. He had to learn by self-discovery and free choice how to live as Son of God. And in so doing he had to fly in the face of everybody's expectations and hopes, except God's. My insistence on the pluralism of spiritualities is not a preface to saying 'but nevertheless there are certain broad lines ...' (in this chapter), or 'but nevertheless I think the following is the best' (in the next chapter). Just the opposite. I want to insist that every person or group has to discover and decide on their own spirituality. God himself is certainly a party to this discovery and decision, but I do not think he dictates them.

I: THE SPIRIT OF GOD

Unity and Diversity

Saul of Tarsus is the person in the New Testament whose development as a person we know most about. He shows clearly how spiritual development, or becoming oneself, is a matter of personal decision. On the road to Damascus, he had an experience that broke up his whole life as he had been living it. That experience set him out on a journey which had no map, except for the suffering, death and resurrection of Jesus Christ. The meeting with the heavenly Jesus, recounted three times in the Acts of the Apostles, released energies in Saul that took him down paths that do not appeal to everybody. Is he too emotional? Doesn't he deal insensitively with women? Could he not write more simply? Should he not have stayed on in Athens rather than moving on to Corinth? Saul became Paul by leaving behind his character as an all-too-predictable Jewish fundamentalist, and becoming fully alive to himself in Jesus Christ. And as Paul, he became very much his own person, someone other people might wish to differ from.

Paul draws more attention than anyone else to the variety of ways in which the Spirit of God leads people to live. There is a diversity of gifts in Christ. There is a diversity of ministries. There is and an abundance of 'fruits of the Spirit', as he calls them. There are different conditions of life: celibate (like him), and married. There are different social conditions, slave and free. There are men and women. There are different nationalities. And though, as he says, 'all are one in Christ Jesus',[2] it is very much a unity in diversity.

The diversity comes from the natural origins and qualities of each person. It also comes from upbringing and the gifts of the Spirit. The unity comes from everyone trying to be faithful to himself or herself, from everyone trying to communicate with other people, and from the three persons in one God: the Spirit, Jesus the Son, and the Father.

Paul calls his readers to imitate him.[3] I do not think by that he intends them to become replicas of himself. What he wants is for everyone, like himself, to respond to the will of God, which is different for everyone. If we need help to discover what the will of God is, as we often do, it is help to discover and respond in a way that is really 'us'. And this inevitably produces a kind of harvest of spiritualities, group and individual spiritualities, fully developed spiritualities and ones that people choose to leave aside .

Is there a fixed, immutable core at the heart of spirituality? There is, namely, human reality and divine reality, in both of which loving freedom walks hand in hand with truth. On the human level, the reality is diverse. A Russian is a Russian, and an African is an African. Men and women are different. Certainly, things like intelligence and sexuality, or affection and sadness, have definite natures that cannot be indefinitely transformed. Despite these basic samenesses, different individual people and their spiritualities are still amazingly diverse. There is a fixed core at the heart of human and divine reality. There is every person's and every society's own particular truth. Only in that sense is spirituality anything fixed. Otherwise, the possibilities for spirituality are unlimited.

Nations and Cultures

A lot of what seems fixed in spiritualities comes, not from human nature or from God, but from nationality and culture. People of different nationalities have value-systems of their own, which form part of the way many people belonging to these nationalities go to God and live for him. Africans, for example, like to live in large open-plan communities, and to express themselves by dancing, while Europeans often prefer privacy and reading. Nationality is not, of course, static. This is especially true in border areas or when travel is easy. In any case, people who belong to the same nation will range from those who are very nationalistic to those who are not. But nationality does tend to create a similar way of doing things, including spiritual things.

Culture is different from nationality, to the point where people, very different in nationality and language, can have broadly the same culture: the universal culture of young people the world over is a clear example of this. But whether a culture is confined to a small group or is worldwide, like nationality it contains value-options. Culture influences how people look at themselves, at one another, and at God. Contemporary Irish people, for example, usually play themselves down, try to say what will please others, and believe in God. These things may change, since culture is not static either, but they will probably change in a particularly Irish way. Cultural change is often something that people can choose or resist, but whichever they do will probably have a strong influence on their spirituality.

I think this is important for understanding one's own spirituality and that of other people. If mocking religion is culturally acceptable, then a person who is determined to remain religious may become aggressive. Or he may become defensive. Or he may become very secure and self-possessed. And if mocking religion ceases to be culturally acceptable, some people, or even many people, may put on the externals of religion without accepting it interiorly.

What emerges from this is that people who are concerned with spiritual living need to pay attention to what is going on, in and around them, on the levels of culture and nationality. What is especially important is not to reduce spirituality to either nationality or culture. Spirituality belongs to the freest and most intimate part of an individual or group, even if it expresses itself in cultural or national forms.

God, gods and no-god

Because spirituality is a person's movement towards God, whether alone or with others, it might seem that belief in God is absolutely fundamental in spirituality. But I do not think this is so. What is absolutely fundamental is honesty or commitment to truth. It is this that leads to the acknowledgement of God. There are, and presumably always will be, people whose love of truth has not yet led them to God, or not to the one God, or perhaps has led them to belief in many gods. I do not see how such people can be excluded from some kind of spiritual living. The ancient Celts, like some Africans to this day, believed in many gods, and this gave them their reverent attitude to nature. One of the main streams of Buddhist religion does not believe in God or in gods, but it is very attentive to the spiritual within the human person. Staying with that need not be unspiritual.

The reality is that there is one God, who created and lives in every part of the world, while being completely other than it, whose Son became a human being, and whose Spirit takes up his abode in human hearts to enable us to live like children of God. People who believe in many gods, and even those who believe in none, can discover and live by fragments of that reality. This is because the true God is so different from anything we can imagine him to be, that moving towards him involves a stage of near-atheism. Sometimes real atheism can come very close to belief in God, and be easily changed into it. A person who is really close to God will find it is not difficult to identify with those who believe in many gods, and with those who, in all honesty, find they cannot believe in any.

Christianity

Christianity confronts people of every cultural and ethnic background with a gospel or 'good news:' that God has become a human being, has suffered and died like us and for us, has risen from the dead, gone to heaven and from there sent the Holy Spirit on the human race. Put in such simple terms, the gospel seems to set aside what I already said about the many spiritualities. Granted that the gospel is true, it might seem that there is only one spirituality. But this does not follow. To begin with, all nationalities and cultures continue in their many-sided developing existence. Moving towards God has always to take account of them. Again, it is possible for us to treat God-who-is-a-man in exactly the same way as we treat the invisible God: we can locate him equally everywhere, or even refuse to recognise him. What God has done is to establish himself in human nature as the intimate companion of every human life, with the words and actions and character of Jesus and the power of the Holy Spirit to guide and inspire everyone. God has entered into the history of the human race, and of every person, and of every group. To each of them he has said: 'You are mine'.[4] God has not done this to colonise us, as it were, but to participate in our life. The gospel makes possible the living of a fully spiritual life. But it does not make everyone live exactly the same spiritual life. The gospel does not in any way diminish the number of spiritualities, embryonic or developed. It does not set up a spiritual empire.

The gospel is not simply a formula of words; it is also a body of people, those who believe in it and are commissioned to transmit it, and a set of sacraments that bring believers into contact with the living Christ. That is to say, the gospel is church, in fact, *a* church. Gospel, in this sense, has a definite nature or structure, like the sexuality, intelligence, affection and sadness mentioned earlier. It also has a definite history. Particular things happened in it and to it, including some things that should not have have happened. The gospel-that-is-church is not something totally flexible and it is not something ideal. It is there for everyone, and yet it offers a different way into itself to everyone. Life's ultimate adventure consists in discovering and living out the way the gospel challenges oneself and one's companions. With all that, the gospel needs to remain a spirituality, not a culture or a programme. The gospel, that is, must be allowed to bring a person closer to himself or herself, to everyone else and to God.

Theologies

Christianity can be stated very simply, as I have tried to do. St Paul is perhaps the person who responded to it most directly in its simplest form: meeting the crucified and risen Christ and receiving his Spirit. But even from the start, Christianity revealed its richness in a certain pluralism. The New Testament presents several quite different approaches to Christ: that of Paul, that of John, that of Luke, that of James, that of the letters to Ephesus and Colosse, and that of the Book of Revelation. There are, we learn, some forty different titles given in the New Testament to Jesus, from 'King of Kings' to 'Rabbi.'[5] This range of difference in approaches to Christianity is sometimes expressed by speaking of different 'theologies' to be found in the New Testament itself. As well as these, different theologies have developed over the past two thousand years, all within the boundaries of Christianity.

To a large extent, theologies and spiritualities go together in matching pairs. For example, a theology which lays great stress on the poverty of Christ as a human being, like that of St Luke, will naturally go along with a spirituality which values a very simple life. On the other hand, a spirituality which tries to accommodate a fairly comfortable life-style may prefer a theology which emphasises Jesus as a wonder-worker. In spite of this link between a spirituality and a like-minded theology, there is a fundamental difference between them. Spirituality takes its starting point from the experience of a person or a group trying to move towards God, while theology seems to start in the mind, with a body of teaching and ideas. Theology and spirituality are very different. Still, they need each other, and every spirituality needs an appropriate theology. Damage is bound to be done if there is not a reasonably close fit between a person's spirituality and his or her theology. Experience shows that not enough attention has always been paid to this point in catechetical or formation programmes, for example, when people are being educated spiritually towards a love of the poor, and at the same time being educated intellectually to regard poverty as something bad. I think that the variety of theologies available today entitles people to be quite free and enterprising in selecting their theology. They can choose the one that best suits their own spirituality, that is, their own spirit. By the same token, great care needs to be taken in selecting the right one. And of course, nobody is free to pick and choose regarding the essentials of the faith.

Churches

There is a diversity of churches to be found in the New Testament. Basically, these are local churches, at Rome, Antioch, Corinth, Jerusalem and so on, but there are also types of churches, those founded by Paul and John for example. Keeping this diversity of groupings together in such a way that they were all recognisably the followers of one Lord, Jesus Christ, led to the development, right from New Testament times, of special structures and ministries: itinerant apostles, the sending of letters, bishops and even the papacy itself.

Groups like individual churches, corresponding to what we would call today parishes or dioceses, are the natural seed-ground for different spiritualities and theologies. For example, one church might have a spirituality and a theology centred on the death and resurrection of Jesus, while another might have one centred on God's incarnation and his birth as a human being. And while there could be all kinds of reasons for this diversity, it might come down to something as simple as the time of year when it was normal for people to have holidays – late spring, for example, or mid-winter. Which would not matter. There are many ways into the mystery of Christ, and in any case each 'way' can and does interact fruitfully with others. The effect of Taizé prayer on Catholic Good Friday worship is a very good example of fruitful interaction.

The multiplicity of churches antagonistic to each other, which has developed principally in the second half of Christianity's history to date, is not something that any spirituality or theology can accept calmly. It is something we shall return to in the concluding part of this chapter, 'Anti-spirituality.'

Jesus Christ, yesterday, today and forever.
Beyond all nations and cultures, religions, theologies, spiritualities and churches, stands the person of Jesus Christ. This, despite the fact that some people give themselves the title 'Christian' while others reject either Christ or Christianity or both – and despite the fact that the majority of the world's five billion and more people have neither heard of Christianity or its founder. The man who was crucified by human beings for proclaiming the fatherhood of God, his own divine sonship and the unity of the human race, and who rose to new life in the power of that gospel, plays the central role in the story of the human race. What he stood for, died for and rose for, is the kernel of what it is to be human. The spirituality of a person or a group stands or falls by its ability to absorb the gospel of Jesus Christ. He is the ultimate in honesty or truthfulness, which is why he so often uses the word 'Amen!' ('In truth! It is so!') and is even called 'the Amen' at one place in the bible.[6] He is also the new Adam,[7] perhaps the only real Adam the human race has known.

Jesus Christ is the supreme model of honesty and truthfulness, and therefore of spirituality. It was these human qualities that helped him to discover his own identity as Son of God. They also led him to understand what it is to be human. That perhaps is why the title he preferred to give himself was 'Son of Man.' His honesty led him to teach what he knew about being Son of God and son of man with extraordinary attractiveness and authority.

He did not mind the opposition he encountered from people entrenched in positions of power. These people killed him, but, because what Jesus taught and lived was true, human death for him meant nothing but entering into his own life as Son of God. His gospel, which his disciples preached and still preach in the power of the Spirit, is that the same life is for everybody, on condition only of discovering and honestly living out who they are. This honesty is not possible without the assistance of divine grace, or the Holy Spirit.

The Holy Spirit

The human qualities of honesty and truthfulness are always impressive. They are often very frightening. 'Humankind can bear very little reality',[8] as the poet says. This perhaps is why the 'power from on high'[9] was needed before the disciples of Jesus could set out to preach his gospel. In fact, in the books called 'the gospels,' Jesus himself received the gift of the Holy Spirit before he began to preach his gospel. He was even conceived in his mother's womb by the power of the same Holy Spirit. All of which shows how dependent people are on the Holy Spirit to be honest with themselves in Christ's way. To insist on autonomy, 'going it alone', is so obviously wrong as to be dishonest.

At the same time, it is striking how the Holy Spirit does not suppress human responsibility. For one thing, his action always respects a person's freedom. The conception of Jesus in the womb of Mary depended entirely on her consent, 'let it happen to me as you have said.'[10] The coming of the Holy Spirit on Jesus at his baptism depended on his making a decision to be baptised by John. The coming of the Holy Spirit on the disciples after the ascension of Jesus depended on their decision to remain together. What is more, the effect of the coming of the Holy Spirit on a person or a group is to set them free to be more fully themselves, not less. Grace, as it is said, perfects nature, it does not destroy it. The effect of the Holy Spirit on a man like Damian of Molokai, or a woman like Teresa of Calcutta, or a nation like the Irish nation, is the preservation and enhancement of what is most truly personal in them. And the freedom remains. It is always possible for an individual or a group to withdraw from association with God's grace. Though a heavy price in dehumanisation has to be paid.

The Holy Spirit was at work in the world long before the coming of Christ. He is still at work even outside Christian circles. He leads people and nations to Christ's unique sense of humanity and of belonging to God's family. I would suggest that wherever there is the combined sense of the fatherhood of God and the brotherhood of humankind, there is the mark of God's Spirit. That deep feeling for the truth of Christ's central teaching (even without knowing whose it is) is the basis of the unity of mankind. But the Holy Spirit's special space for action is inside the church. Within the church there is no limit to the gifts that are given by God's Spirit. They are given in the sacraments. They are given in answer to prayer. And they are given as a reward for the good use of earlier graces.

Psychologies

Spiritualities are, ultimately, at least as numerous as people. But such things as nationality, culture and theology tend to produce types of spirituality. So barriers spring up between spiritualities. A science which, theoretically at least, should do much to break down those barriers is psychology. But there is a plurality of psychologies too. Some branches of psychology have undergone an extremely rapid expansion in the present century. This explosion has had dramatic effects in the field of spirituality. Speaking very generally, psychology has had three effects on spirituality, two negative, one positive.

The first negative effect is that developments in psychology have often concealed some earlier psychological discoveries which spirituality had made its own. One such discovery is the theory of the different powers of the human person (intellect, will, memory, imagination, emotions, and so on.) This theory is often ignored in modern psychology. As a result, it can be difficult for people who grew up with the psychology of today to understand the older spiritualities. Consequently, it is often not easy for us to make contact with some of the greatest geniuses of spirituality the world has known, for example, St John of the Cross.

The second negative effect is that many of the developments in psychology in this century have incorporated ideas which were quite wrong. Most of them were gradually weeded out as the science developed. For example, early twentieth century psychology incorporated strong faith in the reliability of scientific method. Scientists in the second half of the century have grown much humbler about their methods. The trouble is that it was the earlier, more dogmatic and more erroneous psychology, that inflicted most damage on spirituality. One clear example was questioning the value, or even the feasibility, of chastity.

Many of the developments in psychology in recent decades have made it more humane and more moderate. Their effect on spirituality has been highly beneficial, in my opinion. A good example is the way spiritual direction has developed along the lines of Rogerian counselling. It did not, in the process, lose its own essential focus on a person's relationship with God. This kind of spiritual direction, which is in the tradition of St Ignatius Loyola, is proving very helpful to people. It is helping them to be true to themselves and to discover what God is doing in their lives. Other developments of psychology that have benefited spirituality are a more accurate knowledge of mental illnesses, and the understanding of the unconscious mind and its 'defence mechanisms.'

Spiritualities have taken up different attitudes to psychology. Some types of spirituality have remained almost fundamentalist in refusing to have anything to do with psychology. Others have become almost secular and naturalistic by substituting a psychology for openness to God's grace. Others still have managed to strike a balance between openness to grace and awareness of human dynamics. Most modern spirituality, including some of the best, uses a great deal of psychological terminology and theory. And yet, psychology has penetrated our culture so much that the same is true of some of the forms of 'unspirituality' and 'anti-spirituality' currently in circulation.

II: UNSPIRITUALITY

I think that peoples' sense of what it is to be human enables us to recognise spirituality very easily, when divine grace and human honesty come together. I do not think it is any more difficult to recognise what is called 'unspirituality.' It shows in the presence of dishonesty or the absence of any sense of the divine. But there are many kinds of unspirituality. I think it is important to look at some of them.

Sensuality

A sensual person is one who gratifies his or her sensual appetites (for things like praise, drink or food) as often as possible. There can be all sorts of reasons for this. Sometimes the sensual person is more a victim of circumstances than really at fault. Overeating, for instance, can be the result of chronic shame brought about by neglect. But wherever it comes from, sensuality always seeks easy gratification. This prevents a person taking the time to examine a situation carefully. So a sensual person cannot see things as they are. The most he can do is notice the presence or absence of whatever it is he likes. Neither can he always say how things appear to him. That is often too painful, and pain is what the sensual person cannot put up with. So dishonesty tends to go with sensuality.

Seeing all this written down has a strangely old-fashioned look. I think the reason is that an astonishing amount of commerce at the present time is based on pleasant sensations produced by goods offered for sale, or linked with them in advertisements. Not only that, but a huge proportion of what people read or view is paid for by that kind of advertising. Drink and foodstuffs and reading material are promoted in terms of sensual enjoyment. That is what you would expect. But so, surprisingly enough, are pieces of machinery. Television, perhaps because it is the medium which can best mimic reality, seems to carry the most sensual messages. This may be why some of those who have thought most deeply about spirituality today (for example Jean Vanier[11]) take a negative view of television. It certainly looks as if a great deal of modern commerce, and of the media which promote commerce, can only thrive because spirituality has been overshadowed by sensuality.

Sensuality has, of course, always found ways of thriving, even without modern conditions. For this reason, a certain simplicity and even austerity of life has always been favoured by people who wish to cultivate spirituality. And conversely why sensuality is always promoted by those who oppose spirituality. For example, in Calabar, West Africa, during the nineteen-twenties,[12] some people took fright at the progress Christianity was making. So they quite deliberately targeted young people by means of seductive approaches, with some success. To make things more complicated, there is a sort of puritanical anti-sensuality, a pseudo-asceticism, that is just as unspiritual as its opposite. Perhaps what is most important is for individuals, families and local communities to be left with their own capacity intact for deciding how to manage their exposure to sensory stimulation. That is better than having everything decided for them by the remote operators of mass media of communication, of commerce or of public policy.

Love of Money

St Paul quotes a proverb of his time to the effect that love of money is the root of all evils.[13] I may seem to be softening his stand by putting love of money under 'unspirituality' instead of 'anti-spirituality.' Certainly, it can be that, but love of money is at least unspiritual. It takes so much of the good out of things – even a first communion or a confirmation. One of the less happy memories I have of my years in Africa is how, gradually, everything came to have its cash value. Oranges, for example, which traditionally had been left for the children to eat, came to be harvested

for the few coins they brought in. It became harder to ask people
to do the smallest service (for the village community) without
their turning round and asking for *okuk* (money.) There is, of
course, every reason for blaming this degeneration on the inter-
national debt, and so on large-scale money grubbers in the First
World. But the effect on the ground was to move people a step
further away from reality. When I got back to Europe, I was initially shocked when I heard some teenagers expressing their
ideal in life in terms of lots and lots of money. I had to admit, however, that the quick calculator of my own mind was very good at
working out the cash potential of every situation. Religion has a
long history of having its ideals spoilt by love of money. It is for
this reason that movements of religious reform always try to minimise peoples' desire and even need for money. The 'Protestant
ethic', which advocates strict honesty in all financial dealings, is a
case in point, as is the vow of religious poverty. By such means as
these, it is possible to 'make friends of the mammon of iniquity,'[14]
as the gospel puts it. It is even possible to develop a spirituality of
wealth.[15]

Fashion and Routine

Something that can variously be called routine, or fashion, or
even superstition, often prevents us being honest about our own
feelings and opinions. Even as I write, I am conscious of conform-
ing to fixed patterns which take away my spontaneity and give
me an excuse for not really thinking. Fashion, or what used to be
called 'custom', has the same effect. It is usual for people to do
things that would be extraordinary if it wasn't for the fact that
they are often done – smoking, for example, up to recently. I see
both fashion and routine as a kind of superstition. Superstition is
doing things or believing things without examining why. Children and young people are especially liable to get caught in fashion
traps. Fashion, after all, bonds them to their peers. And bonding
to their peers is one of the things they often want very much. But
it does not take much experience, of buying Christmas presents
for example, to see that the natural bonding instinct of young people is being exploited by commercial interests.

It is not, of course, by any means only children who are dead-
ened and unspiritualised by routine/fashion/superstition. Those
in the distribution trade have often very little control about what
to sell. They must follow demand in order to stay in business and
keep their employees in work. It is by no means easy to trace the
infection sources of these de-spiritualising fashions and ideas. I

suspect that even if we could trace them, we would find them difficult to control. The easiest thing is to try to persuade everyone to take full personal responsibility for everything they buy or use or wear or say. A well-known radio-show host advises listeners and viewers of the media to 'answer back' what they hear – retorting 'that's not true.' His advice could be extended to everything life tries to foist on people – 'Answer life back.'

Beginning to live a spiritual life at any age means breaking out of the fashions and patterns and illusions being presented by 'the world'. Beginning to lead a spiritual life means owning one's opinions and feelings. It means living them, or changing them. That can sometimes mean even breaking out of particular religious routines. The key is honesty and one's personal sense of the divine.

III: ANTI-SPIRITUALITY

Unspirituality can be described, in a general way, as missing or ignoring the truth. Anti-spirituality is deliberately accepting falsehood. Sometimes it is vividly described as setting up a false god. I do not think there is any limit to the number of anti-spiritualities that can be set up. It will probably be enough to mention carnality, materialism and irreligion.

Carnality
Some ancient European cultures had gods or godesses of love. Love is an extremely precious thing. But to have a special 'god' for it is to set up a false kind of love. The one God, who created the world and the human race, is the great source and model and object of genuine love. It is not usual these days to set up false gods, but there is a modern successor to the ancient god of love. It can be called 'carnality,' from the Latin word *caro* (meaning flesh). The simple definition of carnality is the doctrine and practice that considers sexual pleasure as an absolute good. This is a falsehood, because sexual pleasure, though certainly good, is only completely good in the setting of married love established by God. Everyone, I think, knows that spontaneously. But it is obscured by the various forms of unspirituality. More seriously, carnality is promoted by an influential neo-pagan lobby.

A person who wants to live a spiritual life must certainly never turn away from affectionate love between people. Or must turn to it. What he or she needs to turn away from is the carnality that falsely separates sexuality from family-founding love. To a large extent, this is something that it is better to do quietly, without making long speeches or even writing long passages in books about it. The option for chastity is the among quietest and most private things a person does. Reserve on this matter seems to be deeply rooted in human nature. But that does not make opting for chastity any less a crucial step.

Materialism

Materialism also proclaims a falsehood: 'only matter matters.' 'Matter' means whatever satisfies a certain range of human desires and whatever can be experienced by the senses. Food and drink are matter. So are the height and weight of a thing. There are many realities that are not matter. Examples are, a smile, a piece of music and the way it is played, patience, and God. A materialist is a person who wants life to be based on things like food and drink and the measurable aspects of things. He does not think that smiles, music, goodness or God enter the equation of life. He (is it always a he?) may be quite tolerant about them. It is just, he says, that they do not really matter.

Materialism is anti-spiritual because it denies the importance of the centre of all spirituality. It ignores the things that communicate something of what God is like, such as music and poetry. It is not interested in the ways in which human beings can come into communication with God, such as grace and goodness and prayer. Essentially, materialism is self-contradictory, because nothing material could exist without God to make it. It would be strange if the creature was more important than the creator. In a mysterious way, materialism also paves the way for massive abuse of the material things it values. The disastrous technology of the atheistic former Soviet Union, and the destruction of the rain forests and the pollution of the atmosphere in the West , are the effects of two equally materialistic systems, economism (a form of capitalism) and communistic materialism.[16]

Materialism holds that 'only matter matters.' The 'only' is important. Every kind of spirituality also holds that matter matters: God created it, and human salvation depends on how we use it. There is little spirituality in a person who uses matter destructively, for example by the way he drives a car, or refuses to use it constructively, for example in the exercise of kindness by feeding some hungry people. Spirituality does not hold that 'matter does not matter'. It holds that matter is very important indeed. What it does not believe is that matter is the only factor of any importance in the equation of life.

Irreligion

By 'irreligion' I mean neglect of God, refusing to give him the respect and reverence that is due to him. Like the other anti-spiritualities I have mentioned, it is based on falsehood. It is based on the double falsehood that God does not want anything from people and that people do not need to pay attention to God. It holds for the complete independence or autonomy of God and the human race. This is not setting up a false god. It is not denying the reality of God or the importance of things that reveal God. It is a kind of apartheid – strict segregation between God and people.

Irreligion contains a grain of truth, inasmuch as it begins from a reaction against excessive religion. There is excessive religion when God is mistakenly believed to have left human beings without any freedom. This is the mistake usually made by fundamentalists of all kinds. There is also excessive religion when everything in life is thought of in religious terms. When people think this, it usually means that they are running away from reality. Irreligion sometimes appears to be justified because excessive religion is so obviously wrong. Whereas in fact irreligion is even more wrong than excessive religion. A balanced religion recognises the respect which God and human beings have for each other. God respects the people he made in his own image. Human beings need to respect and love the God who made them and who alone can satisfy their deepest longings.

Real religion consists in discovering the tender and respectful love which God, on the one hand, and the men and women who know God best, on the other, have for each other. God so 'loved the world [that he] sent his only Son'[17] to be a very lowly member of the human race. The same Son of God, who gave thanks to his Father as Lord of heaven and earth, addressed him by the most tender title of endearment, 'Abba'.[18] These ways of speaking about God do not give any ground for irreligion. In practice, what irreligion is most likely to grow out of is one of the other anti-spiritualities, such as materialism or carnality.

The character of the God, who reveals himself in Christ, is essentially love and kindness, as well as greatness and mystery. This is why the one thing that absolutely must not be found among religious people is hatred and animosity towards each other, or towards anyone. That would be the supreme irreligion. It is the ultimate in anti-spirituality.

Conclusion

Spiritualities are as varied as people and their freedom. From the point of view of inner experience, spirituality consists in a loving response to truth. It consists in accepting the fatherhood of God and the unity of the human family, so far as one can. These restrictions do not limit the variety of spiritualities. What they do is to exclude the various kinds of unspirituality and of anti-spirituality, some of which we have looked at in this chapter. Jesus Christ is the centre of all spirituality, but not as if he deprived human beings of our liberty or devalued us. The very opposite is the case. He is central because he lived and died for the gospel of God's fatherly love for the human family. And, because he is God's only Son, he is the ultimate proof of God's love for people, and of God's desire for each person and group to find out and to be who they are.

Notes

1. Principe, W, 'Pluralism in Christian Spirituality', *The Way*, (Jan 1992) p 54: 'Understood as a person's lived experience, Christian spirituality is completely pluralistic since no two persons live their Christian life in the Spirit in precisely the same way – each person's spirituality is unique and particular.'
2. Galatians 3:28
3. 2 Thessalonians 3:7
4. Isaiah 43:1
5. cf. Bredin, E, *Disturbing the Peace*, Columba Press, Dublin 1985, p 252, remarks that there are 42 such titles. The whole of his Chapter 11, 'Renaming Jesus', is exciting reading.
6. Revelation 3:14
7. Vatican II, Decree on Missionary Activity, n.3; cf. 1 Corinthians 15:45
8. Eliot, T.S, *Four Quartets*, 'Burnt Norton', I, Faber & Faber, London 1975.
9. Luke 24:49
10. Luke 1:38
11. Vanier, Jean, *Community and Growth*, 2nd ed, p 169: 'Television provides images and information and stimulates emotions but cuts people off from relationship.'
12. cf. Cooke, C, *Mary Charles Walker, the Nun of Calabar*, Four Courts Press, Dublin 1980, p 102
13. 1 Timothy 6:10
14. Luke 16:9. *Mammon* is a word in Aramaic, the language spoken by Jesus. It means not only money, but possessions of any kind.
15. St Luke is sometimes called 'the evangelist of the rich'. cf.

Bosch, *Transforming Mission*, Orbis Books, New York 1991, p 103.
16. cf. Pope John Paul II, Encyclical: *Laborem Exercens* (*On Human Work*), n 13, St Paul Publications, NSW 1981, p 53ff.
17. John 3:16
18. Mark 14:36 The closest equivalents in our English are 'dear Father' or a child's 'Daddy'.

CHAPTER THREE

A Spiritual Tradition

Let your good spirit guide me
In ways that are level and smooth
Psalm 142

Christian Gentleness

People often feel the need of belonging to a tradition, even if they do not want their individuality to be suppressed by it. And I think that even original and unconventional people usually do belong to traditions. While Mother Teresa of Calcutta, for example, is unique at the present time, there have always been people like her. They are prophetic people, who love God and love the poor. They invite the world to turn aside into a better way of living.

In this chapter, I am trying to appeal to both groups of people, those who need to belong to a tradition and those who just want to be themselves. I want to present a set of nine men and women who, I think, constitute a tradition. They all broke with the ordinariness of their own time. They did so in ways that have a lot in common. Sometimes the later ones were inspired by the earlier ones. In other cases, there does not seem to have been any particular connection, except a noticeable resemblance in the way they lived and thought, and the fact that all of them have written and been written about. In spite of the embarrassing fact that almost all of them are men, as well as being either priests or monks, all of them without exception have 'the common touch.' I may add that, a bit like Graham Greene's Monsignor Quixote, I owe more to one of the two women than to any of the others mentioned.

I am calling this tradition 'Christian gentleness'. There are other spiritual traditions within the Catholic Church. Some of them would have a good claim to the same title. Still, those words catch the spirit of this tradition particularly well. The various traditions are definitely different from each other, and some of the people I will write about deliberately left other traditions in order to belong to this one. In so doing, they were not despising the other traditions. Rather they were affirming what they knew was right for them. I think that, as a person tries to find his or her own place in life, there has to be a process of preferring and being preferred by one tradition rather than another. Where there is preferring, inevitably there is a kind of rejecting of other things. But this is not

unkind or disrespectful. It is natural, because there is no one spirituality or devotion that suits everyone. As we saw in the last
chapter, while there is an honesty and a truthfulness where all
spirituality comes together, there is also an essential element of
pluralism.

I am presenting just one spiritual tradition here. It is the one I
recognise as mine. Many other people in various countries and
down through the centuries have recognised it as theirs. Local
churches and church institutions have heard it saying something
to them. Even people who prefer other spiritual traditions have
learned from it, as this tradition has learned from others. I will
begin by introducing the individual people who represent the
spiritual tradition of Christian gentleness. Then I will take a more
personal look at the main characteristics of this tradition.

Gregory the Great to L'Arche
Gregory the Great (540-604) was not a priest when he was elected
pope at the age of fifty, much against his will. He had already
proved his worth as governor of the city of Rome and as papal
representative to the court of the emperors at Constantinople. As
pope, he was an extremely wise pastor. He wrote a book called
The Pastoral Rule (or *Pastoral Care*) as a guide for bishops. St
Columbanus, the great Irish missionary of the time, said that the
book was 'sweet as honey'. It did more, perhaps, than any other
piece of writing to promote a firm yet humane and kind spirit in
the Catholic Church throughout Europe. For this reason, I think it
is right to see Gregory as the founder of the spiritual tradition of
Christian gentleness. It has been written of Gregory that 'his teaching became the chief source of medieval spirituality'.[1] He was certainly the person who most influenced St Bernard, and through
him, as well as directly, the spiritual mentors who came afterwards.

There are many things about Gregory's writing that are very
striking. He shows a great love of scripture. He can also turn a
powerful phrase, as for instance when he says that the pastor
'should be very close to everyone in sympathy, and far above
everyone in contemplation.'[2] Gregory's love of scripture and his
effective style go a long way to explaining his influence, but his
real secret is something deeper. It is his extraordinary moderation, his deep sympathy for peoples' feelings. As pope, he regularly
took the side of the poor and unfortunate. His *Pastoral Rule* shows
how closely he felt pastors should identify with the poor. Everyone, he teaches, is equal, even if some are superior by what he

calls 'the accident of power.'[3] The poor are to be offered comfort, while the rich are to be threatened, says Gregory. Though he adds that in this matter care is needed, as 'the rich man may be humble and the poor man proud.'[4] In chapter after chapter of his book, he offers suggestions which are as valid today as in his time. They concern how the pastor is to treat people of all kinds: intelligent and dull, impatient and patient, simple and crafty, sick and well. In all cases, Gregory shows deep concern for human weakness.

Behind this sensitivity lies a sense of what pastoral care is all about, a sense of faith. For Gregory, Jesus Christ is above all the truth, especially the truth about how to live. Living according to the truth leads to an eternal life of happiness when this life is over. For Gregory, Jesus is the truth, and God is boundless light. This has led one author to say of him that 'the form of his spiritual teaching [is] one of knowledge rather than union...'[5] I think that here we touch on something very fundamental in the spiritual tradition of Christian gentleness. The tradition seeks God, and indeed everything else too, principally in a kind of knowing. But this knowing is sensitive. It is shaped by feelings about the things that are known. In this tradition, a clear mind and a sensitive heart work together to reach union with God and all that he has created.

What has been said about Gregory's idea of faith is a good illustration of this point:

> It is not in seeing, then, that the vision of faith consists, but in looking with love and a great longing to see. It is not merely a knowledge of God, an act of understanding, but an act of love by which we possess the divine truth ...[6]

In this tradition, we live for God by knowledge. That is, we try to express, especially in words, what we see and feel about God. True, we will only be able to experience God fully in heaven. But it is a fundamental belief of Gregory's that expressing what we know about God greatly enriches life on earth.

Bernard of Clairvaux (1090-1153) was a highly talented person. With several of his brothers and twenty-five other companions, he entered the newly founded Cistercian order at the age of twenty-two. They chose this order so that they could live fully for God. Bernard himself made such spiritual progress that all who knew him considered him a saint. Although he suffered all his life from severe ill-health, nothing mattered more for Bernard than the mystery of Jesus Christ.

What did the mystery of Jesus Christ mean for Bernard? It

meant a very genuine love for gospel values. It meant a deep affection and respect for people. It also meant preaching the Second
Crusade for the protection of the world order he knew and loved.
Bernard's contribution to the tradition of Christian gentleness did
not include pacifism. But it was, nevertheless, a real contribution,
and it depended to no small extent, like Gregory's, on his ability
to communicate. He was not bitter in what he wrote or said. In a
long dispute he had with the theologian Peter Abelard, who
opposed much of what he stood for, people criticised Bernard for
being too moderate.

What Bernard stood for behind his moderation was called
'monastic theology.' That means a way of speaking and writing
about God where the line between prayer and the development of
ideas is very often crossed and re-crossed. His opponent, Abelard,
stood for a more logical and less prayerful approach to the knowledge of God. The other writers in the tradition of Christian gentleness follow Bernard on this point.

They also followed Bernard in the importance they attached to
humility. By this he means 'a most true knowledge of self by
which man becomes lowly in his own sight.'[7] Humility is not by
any means an unhealthy shame or self-dislike. It is a grateful recognition of how much we depend on God and on other people,
and of the fact that they are there for us. Bernard's appreciation of
humility is, I feel, his greatest contribution to our spiritual tradition.

Teresa of Avila (1515-1582) also valued humility. She was a
woman completely without illusions about human nature, and
completely without cynicism. As a young woman, she entered a
convent, but it was only after twenty years, when she was forty,
that she woke up to the reality of her religious commitment. Teresa
discovered the happiness of a fervent spiritual life for herself, and
many other people were glad to share that kind of life with her.
She travelled all over Spain founding small monasteries with
meagre financial resources, where women could live a very
human kind of life for God. Her superiors ordered her to write
down her experience of that life, and the resulting books, especially
her *Life* and *The Interior Castle*,[8] show how living spiritually is
within the reach of ordinary human beings, outside monasteries
as well as inside. Teresa recognised that her own education was
limited, and so she invited John of the Cross to be her theologian
and to work with her. Nevertheless, the church honours Teresa,
like John, with the title of Doctor.

John of the Cross (1542-1591) is another attractive person. His impoverished mother brought him and his two brothers up after his father's early death. He was skilful with his hands, as a carpenter, tailor, painter and bricklayer. Most of all he was deeply attracted to God. John joined Teresa of Avila in renewing the Carmelite order. He became one of those who contributed most in the Europe of his day to recognising the path by which God draws people to himself. John knew great personal suffering, both from ill-health and persecution. His outstanding discovery was that, even in the darkest experiences, there is a brightness that enables people to grow closer to God. Though he spent his own life mostly among the members of his community, what he learned from his experience has proved invaluable to millions of people who were (and are today) leading active lives outside monastery walls.

Among those influenced by Teresa and John of the Cross[9] were a Bishop from Savoy, now part of France, and a priest from the south-west corner of France, Francis de Sales (1567-1622) and Vincent de Paul (1581-1660). St Francis de Sales wrote two books, one of which, *The Introduction to the Devout Life*, ranks with St Gregory's *Pastoral Rule* as a handbook of the spiritual tradition of Christian gentleness. It was translated into many languages, including Irish. St Vincent, on the other hand, wrote only letters and a rule for his missionaries, though his fellow-workers wrote down the talks he gave them.

Francis de Sales' basic contribution to spirituality, or 'devotion' as he called it, was to re-emphasise that spirituality is for everyone. His book on the devout life expresses in simple and gentle terms how people can become more spiritual. The book is written in a style quite like that of Gregory, and is full of wise and humane advice. God, Francis teaches, is the great goal of human life. He describes living for God in terms of the ladder which Jacob saw in his dream.[10] Spirituality is a ladder reaching from earth to heaven, which people go up towards God in prayer and come back down to serve other people. The uprights of the ladder are the love of God and the sacraments that confer it. Francis emphasises the sacraments, whose importance could be taken for granted by Gregory, Bernard and John of the Cross, because the Protestant questioning of that aspect of traditional Christianity made it necessary to be explicit about them. What Francis shows is that the point of the sacraments, and of all other aspects of spirituality, is to enable us to help and to be patient with one another.

Vincent de Paul stands out as 'a model for men of action'. However, he developed the spiritual tradition of Christian gentleness in one vital respect. That is his teaching on humility, and his related teaching that Christianity proves itself by love for the very poorest people. Perhaps no once since St Francis of Assisi spoke so warmly of 'the Lady Poverty' as Vincent did. So far as I know, no one before Vincent spoke so warmly of the great privilege of serving poor people, whom he called 'his lords and masters.' This theme comes to predominate in two of our last three representatives of the spiritual tradition of Christian gentleness.

John Bosco (1815-1888) was born near Turin, capital of the historical region of Savoy to which Francis de Sales also belonged. He set out deliberately to recreate the spirit of his fellow-countryman in the changed conditions of the industrial revolution. This is why he gave to the order he founded the name 'Salesians' (the Society of St Francis de Sales). He also wrote a biography of Vincent de Paul. More than any other priest until the priest-workers of today's France, John Bosco put into practice the ideals of dedication to poverty and the poor. The schools he and his followers founded are marked by deep religious faith and the cultivation of technical skill – an echo of John of the Cross can be heard in that. With John Bosco, our tradition enters the modern largely secularised world.

For John, Christ is above all the teacher of wisdom. Knowledge is the path that leads to God. In addition, joy and the search for human fulfilment are very important for John. One of his favourite quotations from scripture was: 'I know there is no happiness for a human being except in pleasure and enjoyment through life.'[11] Salesian spirituality can be fairly summed up as the pursuit of knowledge and happiness, both centred on Christ.

Thérèse Martin (1873-1897) was one of a number of women who were to make a deep impression on the European mind in the twentieth century, along with such people as Anne Frank, Simone Weil and Vera Brittain. Her external life was short and in no way unusual. But the inner life revealed in her autobiography, *Story of a Soul*, shows great liveliness, faith and kindness. What she stands for is the mystery of the ordinary. She shows how the whole kingdom of God is waiting to be constructed and explored in every human life. Thérèse became a Carmelite nun at the age of fifteen, by which time she had already done much spiritual growing up. Right from the start of her convent life, she aimed at living for the love of Christ and of those who lived under the same roof with her. She offered her life as a sacrifice to God particularly on behalf of missionaries. Her affectionate nature and the directness of her writing made a great impact on the outside world. But, like Bernard and Vincent, the secret of Thérèse's attractiveness is the conviction she had of her own littleness in relation to God. God wanted to achieve a vast amount with her help. She knew it depended on accepting her insignificance. Being humble, in her experience, is not easy, and recognising that is part of humility. Thérèse writes:

> To continue to remain always poor and powerless, there lies the difficulty! Actually, where can we find one who is truly poor? Is not he truly poor who is so humble-minded that he believes himself to be nothing? Oh! let us remain far away from all that is vain-glorious! Let us love our littleness, our lack of sensitivity. We shall then be poor in spirit and Jesus will care for us, however far we may be from him, and will set us afire with his love. [12]

What is often called Thérèse's 'Little Way' is really the path of humility and of absolute trust in God.

Thérèse is not the only person to speak to the twentieth century of the huge spiritual potential of ordinary people. Others include Frank Duff (1889-1980), who founded the Legion of Mary, and Joseph Cardijn (1882-1967), who founded the Young Christian Workers. The person who speaks most powerfully for the spiritual tradition of Christian gentleness, as the century draws to its close is, I believe, Jean Vanier.

Vanier, like Gregory the Great for most of his life, is not a priest. He is a lay Catholic, a Canadian by nationality, a former naval officer who made a study of philosophy. He was born in 1928. He has discovered an amazing way of living Christianity: by forming communities of handicapped and non-handicapped people who live together on terms of complete equality. These communities are called *Communities of L'Arche* (The Ark) and the first and best-known of them is at Trosly-Breuil in France. The best-known account of the spirituality of *L'Arche* is Vanier's book, *Community and Growth*. It is already recognised as a classic. Like the monasteries and religious communities to which most of the other representatives of our tradition belonged, *L'Arche* has generated a spirituality that can enliven a family or any other group of people living together.

My own awareness of the *L'Arche* movement and its significance dates from a visit I made some twenty years ago to Annecy, in France. Annecy is the place where Francis de Sales lived when he was Bishop of Geneva, which was in his time under the control of Calvinists. His grave is in Annecy. On my visit there, I was standing in the cathedral grounds looking towards the lake, across the city, which was crowded with tourists. One unusually lively group of tourists caught my eye. There were nine or ten of them, all chattering together as they moved through the crowd, pointing things out to each other and obviously enjoying themselves. It was only when I looked closely that I saw that they were all handicapped people. At the time I had never heard of *L'Arche*. When I did hear of it soon afterwards, I realised that the group who made such an impression on me must have been from somewhere like that. It was only much later again, when I met people who had lived in *L'Arche* communities and read *Community and Growth*, that I saw the close resemblance between their spirituality and that of Christian gentleness.

Vanier's spirituality, as I read it, is based on two ideas: the insecurity of modern life, and the strength that comes only from faith and love of God. Young people today, he writes,

> are faced with different alternatives: on the one hand insecurity, with all the anguish that implies, or the false securities of work and power, of worldly values and closed-up sects; or on the other hand, being part of a community where they can find themselves and grow into openness and universal love.[13]

The question, he says, for every person and community,

> is how to become rooted in the soil of one's faith and one's identity, in one's own community, and at the same time to grow and give life to others, and to receive life from them.[14]

Community and Growth is a kind of handbook for living in such a community. It expresses the essential broadmindedness and moderation of the tradition beginning with Gregory the Great. Vanier's moderation comes across when he writes, for instance, of the gifts of community, from the gift of authority to the gift of the poor: 'It is often the poorest person – the one who bears a handicap or who is ill or old – who is the most prophetic.'[15] His love of people who are poor shows on every page.

What Vanier writes about meals is a good illustration of how he belongs to the tradition of Christian gentleness:

> Eating well does not mean eating expensively. There is a lot of good food that is cheap too. It is a question of creativity, of culinary skill, especially with the sauces – think of spaghetti without sauce! A sauce is a gesture of *gratuité* [one of his words, which people usually do not try to translate: it means generosity and kindness]. A community which eats nothing

but plain pasta 'because it's cheaper to buy in bulk' will never be a very cheerful place.[16]

Vanier shows how close he is to the deepest aspects of Christian gentleness when he writes about the eucharist and the priesthood. He values the priesthood especially as a sacramental ministry, and one of spiritual guidance, though he does not see the latter as confined to priests. 'The priest's essential responsibility is for the sacramental life of the members of the community, in particular the transforming of bread and wine into the body and blood of Christ. The priest is ultimately linked to the eucharist. Our *L'Arche* communities are always in need of these priest-shepherds who bring the nourishment of the eucharist and the gift of forgivenness ... But they must be men of prayer, transparent, gentle and yet firm, and sometimes even bold in the struggle against the power of darkness and evil. And, by the word they preach, they must remind us constantly how the Body of Christ in the eucharist calls us to see the Body of Christ in the broken bodies of the poor.'[17] For Vanier, the lay person, as for Gregory the Great, a late-comer to orders, the priesthood is vitally necessary, but it is even more necessary for priests to be pastors at heart.

In the rest of this chapter, I will try to describe the Christian gentleness tradition by reflecting on experience. It is usual for writers in this tradition to depend more on experience than on learning, even though learning is something for which they have great regard.

The God of Boundless Light

Gregory's description of God as 'boundless light' speaks strongly to me. It speaks of brightness and space, of freedom and hope. It keeps unlocking new doors as life proceeds. The churches where I attended Mass as a child were the highest buildings around, and the churches' ceilings were as high as their roofs. The daylight came in through extraordinary pictorial windows, most of all above the altar where the Mass took place. The God my parents and the priests and teachers talked about was the most remarkable being we ever heard of. The first thing we learned about him at school was that he made the world. The sense I picked up, and I think all of us did, was that he was our God, as well as our being his, and that it was our world as well as his. We knew all about how big the world was and even the universe, and we felt we belonged there. To travel to a strange city for a football match, or a foreign country for a camp, was simply exploring our space, given to us by our God. Not that most or any of us thought much about

God or religion. Quite the contrary, in fact, with all the other things we had to explore. But religion imparted a sense of boundless space and of brightness waiting to dawn on everything.

Brightness, and even boundlessness, took on a new dimension as evil began to make its presence felt. Initially nothing was particularly bad except insofar as we were told that certain things were bad. But gradually, lies and trickery and stealing and hostility showed their problematic side. That happened when they came to be seen as things other people did to me, as well as my doing them to them. Sexual obsession began to reveal its unacceptable side as something one couldn't just walk away from but dug itself in. As experience developed in this way, the values which society and my peers accepted, particularly religion, began to show their real worth as ways for getting rid of evil. Truthfulness and honesty and other moral qualities were things that shone brightly in comparison with bad living. They offered freedom and the feeling of being good. The sacraments of the eucharist and penance and confirmation proved themselves as sources of the boundless light. Consequently, we saw God as the ultimate source from which that light came.

To a large extent, this vision, carefully guarded by family and teachers and preachers and by myself, was enough to keep me moving forward for many years. But with time, it became clear that the simple ideas of youthful wisdom were giving way to a totally new outlook, even more boundless and bright. Lives begun and lived with old but over-simple certitudes began to collapse into ill-health, broken relationships, loss of faith, the discovery of retarded personal growth, a profound shift in attitudes regarding sexuality and the value of this life compared with the next. God, at this point, is beginning to shine for me with a different brightness, or rather a glow, from parts of myself and of the world that I either ignored or did not know about before. The affective side of people, always honoured in the Sacred Heart devotion, now presents itself as territory simply demanding to be explored. Today a new generation, which has grown up in a different world from mine, is there inviting me to listen to it and to speak into it. Other cultures are inviting me to visit them, to live in them, to share them and to let them share me. For these journeys of exploration, there is nothing I can take with me except myself as I have been and as I am coming to be, and Jesus Christ in the simple but illuminating words of the gospel and in the sacraments. But I have the sense that these will be plenty.

Pastoral Care

I find my identity, to a very large extent, as a close associate of those whom Jesus sent out to preach the gospel to all nations. Most of my time is spent with other people who see themselves in the same light, or who wish to. I am in this line because in my late teens I could not imagine that there was anything more important to do, or anything I wanted more to do. And though I now have a clearer idea of how mixed my motives were then, I still hold the view with which I started out. There is, I am certain, a task of the greatest importance, which consists in bringing to people the gospel taught by Jesus Christ, the Son of God. But God is as much present and alive in the people receiving as he is in me giving, as much or more. What there is for me at present is a deep realisation of how much has changed, and of how much I am being called by Jesus Christ to change in order to get and to remain in touch with his people. People still require the pastoral care which Gregory, Bernard, Francis, Vincent and John Bosco provided, and which Vanier values so highly. No doubt it is still sufficiently the same as it always was for me to learn from the old writers. Still, it is also breath-takingly new.

As far as my experience and reading go, what is new about pastoral care today is its being a three-way personal relationship in which the pastor is listening to God, to himself, and to whoever he is caring for. Principally, pastoral authority is something in the area of personal relationships. It is not a function or position authorising a person to sign certain documents. But, if the pastor is not trying to remain in contact with God, then the care is not really pastoral. If he or she is not in contact with himself or herself, then it is not going to be care – more harm will be done than good. The most pastoral man I knew was an old African Catholic bishop, who had lived through a war and stayed at his post when almost everyone else ran, who had his share of difficult people of different races to deal with, and who was well aware of his own shortcomings. He was unfailingly courteous, he listened, he said clearly what he thought should be done and what he insisted would be done, and he genuinely tried to pray. Life was not easy for him nor did everything under his care go beautifully. But the pulse-beat of Christian life was clearly to be felt, parish by parish, in his diocese. Authority is not always exercised perfectly, but something very important is happening when it is exercised with a good heart.

It is striking how much the writers in our tradition value past-

oral authority. They insist, by word and example, on taking responsibility seriously. Everyone needs someone to take care of
him or her, especially perhaps those inclined to be completely in-
dependent. And yet everyone needs to be taken care of differently,
whence Gregory's saying that pastoral care is the art of arts.[18] Vincent de Paul used to say that anything that went wrong in a community was the superior's fault. Vanier is more explicit:

> Leaders of a community have a double mission. They must
> keep their eyes and those of the community fixed on what is
> essential … They must give direction so that the community
> does not get lost in small wrangles … But the leader's mis-
> sion is also to create an atmosphere of mutual love, confi-
> dence, sharing, peace and joy among the community's mem-
> bers … Human beings grow best in a relaxed atmosphere
> built on mutual confidence. When there is rivalry, jealousy,
> and suspicion, and when people are blocked against each
> other, there can be no community, no growth, no life of wit-
> ness.[19]

I feel sure that there is no association, however small or large,
to which this does not apply. The only thing I would wish to add
is that leaders too can be blocked, perhaps by those who would
like to be leaders but are not, so that everyone has their part to
play in giving the leaders scope. Sometimes this needs as much
skill and personal balance as actual leadership does. The Irish
missionary Columbanus is a good example of this. He protested
vigorously to Gregory the Great at the way the traditions of the
Celtic churches were being swept aside in favour of traditions
that had their origin in Rome.[20] But at the same time Columbanus
recognised unquestioningly the office and the authority of the
pope, and his great personal worth as a pastor. He expresses his
admiration for one of Gregory's books and asks for copies of the
others. It is not only important people who need to treat one another with tact and respect, however. Everybody, whether in the
position of a Gregory or a Columbanus, or at the foot of the ladder,
has his or her own inner authority. It always needs to be used
with moderation and sensitivity.

Poverty and the Poor
When I first began to follow my vocation, I resolved, in a rather
crazy way, to be most exact in observing every regulation, and
above all to be most exact in everything concerning money. I say
'in a rather crazy way' because it is natural for young people to go
to extremes, whatever they are up to, and I was no exception. So

today I find that I have retained the same ideals, only now I know much better what is really essential, and what is not. What is really essential is to try to make God's love known in everything I do, and to identify as much as possible with poor people. Not indeed that I can claim to have made much progress to date, but at least the mist is beginning to clear and the objectives are coming into view. I will mention some things I have found from experience.

As often as possible, I travel by bus, even on long journeys. It is economical and people who are not well off travel that way. What is more, the bus is a great leveller – it's as if people who are travelling as cheaply as possible are a community with no secrets from each other. They communicate with each other in a very natural and relaxed way. I am amazed at how often I, and everyone else on a bus, have shared an episode from someone's life which few fiction-writers could equal for pathos: a woman travelling with a little girl on what was to have been their family holiday, only her husband had to stay behind to look for their elder girl who went missing the night before near a hang-out for drug addicts; a driver being infinitely patient with a very wounded person who had neither ticket nor bus pass; a Polish man who was forced to fight first on one side and then on the other in the Second World War. On these journeys, it is not just that I felt somehow closer to the lives of the people than my ordinary occupations often allow me to be. In a mysterious way, Christ himself seems to be sharing the experiences, the same Christ whose sharp eye for detail, and sympathy for people in their situations, come out in the parables he tells. There is an indefinable sense of being somehow on holy ground when sharing closely with people.

The other thing I have learnt is that I am only on really solid ground in a conversation when I am trying to stay with people on a feeling level. Not necessarily very deep feelings, or religious feelings, but just whatever the feelings are. People need to be sure that the person they are talking to is trying to stay with whatever feelings they are putting out – not prying into uncommunicated ones. It is all very simple, really, just a matter of being present to people. All that has to be done is to check bad habits of being absent from them. Simple though that may be, it is not always easy. There is a strong tendency in middle-class society to distance oneself from personal contact. That is where public transport comes to the rescue, and there are geniuses in the art of being present to others to be met on journeys. I sometimes wonder if cheap travel is not the ideal antidote to television, where the relationships on display can be quite phoney.

The trouble about being poor, even to a limited extent, is that you can get left behind at bus stops, or regarded as a bit of a fool, or associated in in people's minds with those who get blamed when things are stolen. Such experiences are not pleasant, but they do have an advantage that outweighs that. They help one to become a little more humble. Not that they need break your spirit, though being poor can do that. It is the opposite that should happen. Galling experiences throw you back on the resources of your own spirit. They help you to find some real personal strength. That happens on the purely natural level – it is just having the corners knocked off. At a deeper level, these experiences also help one to find common ground with Jesus Christ. His parents could only find a stable for his birth. His relatives thought him a fool. He ended his life crucified between two convicted robbers. The experiences that go with real poverty help us to claim Christ's strength as well as our own. Poverty leads to humiliation, and humiliation leads to humility, and humility consists in claiming our own real personal strength. For this reason, I do not find it surprising that the masters of our spiritual tradition set so much store by poverty and the poor.

Human Values

Our tradition also attaches considerable importance to excellence. Vincent de Paul expressed this in one way by telling his collaborators that the poor were their 'lords and masters'. He insisted that the work of serving them must not be done in a slipshod way. Preaching to poor people required more care, not less, than preaching to the better-off.

Excellence is very evident in the writing of those I am presenting as representatives of the spiritual tradition of Christian gentleness. Without exception, they write with a clarity and a directness, with an intelligence and an emotional warmth that comes through very strongly, even in translations from Latin, French, Spanish or Italian into English. To some extent, this is due to a conscious effort at writing well. It is due also to their being sure about what they wanted to say and having real respect for the people they were writing for. Obscure and unattractive writing nearly always comes from the writer's lack of clarity or lack of conviction about what he is saying, or a certain sense of superiority to his readers. While writing is indeed a technical skill like singing or speaking, technical ability will not make up for any lack of the human qualities of clearmindedness or kindness, especially in writing about spiritual matters.

Human values go beyond those that make for good communication. There are several other values that people need to have, and that need a mention in this context to balance what would otherwise be an excessive emphasis on poverty and humility. I am thinking particularly of a group of qualities that go under the name 'justice' and another group of qualities that go under the name 'courage.'

Just people are honest, straightforward and trustworthy. If they are teachers or a managers, they will probably be regarded as fairminded. Even if people fear them, they will also respect them. People who are just are also truthful, but they show respect for people's feelings – that is, they know how to avoid being brutally truthful. They value social justice, and aim at seeing that organisations they are connected with work together for the good of all, members and non-members alike. And finally, people who are just like to see procedures properly carried out and records properly kept, as much as can reasonably be expected. It is interesting that all the representatives of the Christian gentleness tradition we have considered held responsible positions and could be relied upon.

Courage is something of a corrective to the cool reasonablness of justice. It is what puts fire and enthusiasm into the way a job is done. I think that when individuals or associations begin to fail, it because their courage is going. The will to face difficulties and to solve them is no longer there. The desire to make one's mark, or to make one's mark again, is gone. The four qualities traditionally associated with courage, namely, magnanimity, magnificence, patience and perseverance,[21] are a great advertisement and morale-booster for any group or person. Being able to think big and to bounce back are likely to attract members for groups and disciples for individuals. In the tradition we are considering, not only are the poor served and humility practised, but both are done with impact and style. In spiritual living there is what John of the Cross calls an 'ardent boldness.'[22]

Charity

A spirit of great kindness and simple love of people is another notable feature of the tradition I am presenting. In one way, this is one of the human values of the tradition, and surely the most important. It is however more than a human value: there is something specifically Christian about it. Love is, in St Paul's words, 'poured out in our hearts by the Holy Spirit.'[23] It is, I think, one of the strangest things about Christianity as a whole, let alone this particular spiritual tradition, that the thing which is most divine about it is also the most human. The strict meaning of the word 'charity' is this human/divine love.

Personally, I find it impossible to point to any part of the Christian code of love and say 'that is purely and specifically Christian', as if nobody except a Christian could be expected to admire it or to try to fulfil it. In fact, I believe that if we understand ourselves aright, Christianity is the least sectarian of religions. Jesus's reduction of the commandments to two, love of God and love of neighbour, means just that. The account of the Last Judgment, which crowns St Matthew's gospel, teaches simple humanity: 'whatever you do to the least of my brothers, that you do unto me.'[24] And so I have come to the personal conclusion that the only thing that could possibly be called specifically Christian about love is, that Christians are empowered actually to be kind and patient and generous. I would even risk saying say that the whole point of the coming of God into our world is to enable people to live the law of love. And I am not aware of any spiritual tradition within Christianity that does not have love as its main rule of action.

What I am aware of is that practically everything in my experience tends to drive me away from keeping the law of love. So many things I want to do stem from self-interest or even self-indulgence. I think the whole of economic life stems from those, at present, rather than from the principle of justice (and so of love), 'give everyone what is due to them.' Worse again, self-interest and self-indulgence do not even add up to a reasonable love of self, but only to scoring points in a particular game, (the success game, the money game, and so on). John Bosco was right to push people back to asking what they really needed to make them happy. Real love for oneself and for others involves satisfying real needs and wants. Our problem is having so many artificial needs, which drive us away from ourselves, and from other people who seem to be in competition with us. Keeping the better-off at the level they think is their right necessitates keeping a large proportion of the world's population in a state of unbelievable deprivation. And not only the population of the world as a whole, but of each country too. In the case of Ireland, 'far too frequently, the pursuit of individual and sectional gain has taken precedence over working towards the wider goal of developing the economic resources of this island for all its citizens.'[25] Can it be denied that the sheer cost of employing anybody is one of the main reasons why so many people have no work? But I experience fierce resistance within myself to the idea of a radical change in my way of thinking or acting, so as to give a fair deal to other people. That, and not the theory of the matter, is the problem about charity.

The eucharist is the central celebration of love amongst Christians. In it, Christ gives himself to his people under the form of bread and wine. Sometimes people feel their faith threatened by the fact that there is no perceptible change in the bread and wine after the eucharistic consecration. My own view is that this is God's way of saying to us that the perceptible side of the change is not supposed to be in the eucharistic food but in the communicants. The eucharist calls for and makes possible the practice of love, both on the personal and the social level. The real threat to people's faith is when charity doesn't happen. Love is the decisive test of any spirituality.

Prayer and Action

It is a feature of the tradition we are considering to insist that there is a strong bond between prayer and action. This might seem to be one of its most attractive points. In reality, it opens the way to the greatest risk faced within this spiritual tradition. That is the risk of activism or of considering prayer chiefly as a prelude to action. The trouble with action is that there is something ambiguous about it. Action can mean anything from the most kindly and well-planned programmes for the relief of misery to putting ill-conceived or unjust schemes into practice. The way the church itself and individual Christians, even a Gregory or a Bernard, have sometimes been compromised by political involvement, is a good example of the dangers of insisting too much on the unity of prayer and action. And yet, if prayer is taken seriously enough, and people are careful to make sure that the action in question deserves to be linked with prayer, then the idea that prayer should lead to action is valid.

The kind of prayer taught in our tradition is *meditation*, which happens in three stages. First, responding to God's revelation or some part of it by paying careful and reverent attention to it, for example, the words of the Father concerning Jesus, 'This is my beloved Son, listen to him.' Second, letting oneself become affectively involved in what is being prayed about: amazement at the truth that God became a human being, or gratitude to God for it, or shame at our lack of faith, or the desire that God should increase our faith. The third stage is considering what demands this may make on one's practical commitment, in present circumstances, and asking God's guidance on this point. This could lead to anything from learning more about one's faith, to breaking some habit

that is unworthy of the faith, to embarking on a political programme.

The essential thing in this way of praying is, I think, that the
three stages should follow in that order. First, an open-minded listening to what God is saying. Second, allowing the free movements of one's own heart to respond to what God says. And only
then considering what course of action God's word, and our inner
response to it, point out. What is to be done is not determined
beforehand. It emerges from meditation with mind and heart on
what God has revealed. The aim in prayer is to follow where God
directs us, not to enlist the aid of the Almighty in what we have
already decided to do.

The most important stage in this kind of meditation is the second. Deep-seated resistance to God's word often arises within
ourselves, and it is dealt with in the second stage of meditation.
We find we have wrong motives for doing what we think God
wants, or even for doing what he really does want; or we find that
we do not want to do what he is asking us to. For example, people
praying about entering the priesthood may come to realise that
they have some unacceptable reasons for wanting to become a
priest. The assistance of a spiritual guide is often needed at this
stage. He or she can help us to recognise facts about ourselves or
God or life in general that are not easy to accept.

This strong bond between prayer and action is a valuable aspect of the Christian gentleness tradition. It prevents spirituality
becoming a sort of spiritual pastime. Prayer leads to putting into
effect the plans of God.

Renewing Tradition
Most people only realise the value of their tradition when they are
faced with handing it on to a new generation. They find themselves saying, in words which they heard from their own parents
and teachers, why certain things are important. They hear and see
the questions of their own childhood and youth in the faces of the
new generation. Young people challenge their elders to be faithful
to their tradition. It is not a challenge that everyone can face suc-
cessfully. Holding on to the externals of the tradition helps. But
the only sure way of meeting the challenge is to accept the inner
spirit of the tradition. For that, a person needs to be creative, and
add his or her own original contribution to the tradition. In order
to accept a tradition so that it can be passed on, it is necessary to
give oneself to it.

Notes

1. Leclercq, J, *The Spirituality of the Middle Ages*, Burns & Oates, London 1968, p 3.
2. 'The Book of Pastoral Rule of Saint Gregory the Great, Roman Pontiff, to John, Bishop of the City of Ravenna', in Schaff & Wace, eds, *A Select Library of Nicene and Post-Nicene Fathers*, reprinted Eerdmans, Grand Rapids 1969,Vol XII, p 12. [I have simplified the translation here, to catch the freshness of the original.]
3. The same, p 14.
4. The same,p 25
5. Leclercq, work cited, p 29.
6. The same, p 26f.
7. St Bernard, *On the degrees of humility and pride*, ch 1, n 2.
8. cf. Leclercq, Talbot & Rochais, eds, *Sancti Bernardi Opera*, Editiones Cisterciences, Rome 1957-1977, vol 3, p 17.
9. cf. *The Collected Works of St Teresa of Avila*, 3 vols, trs Kavanaugh, K. & Rodriguez, O, Institute of Carmelite Studies, Washington 1976-1985.
10. cf. Flanagan,E, 'The Carmelite dimension in St Vincent and its implications today,' *Colloque*, [Journal of the Irish Province of the Congregation of the Mission], n 17, Vincentian Community, Dublin 1988.
11. Francis de Sales, *An Introduction to the Devout Life*, ed Peter Toon, Hodder & Stoughton, London 1988, p 25.
12. Qoheleth 3:12
13. Quoted from her letters in Jamart, *Complete Spiritual Doctrine of St Thérèse of Lisieux*, Alba House, New York 1961, p 51.
14. Vanier,J. *Community and Growth*, DLT, London 1989, p 4.
15. The same, p 6f.
16. The same, p 262.
17. The same, p 324f.
18. The same, p 247.
19. *The Pastoral Rule*, Ch 1, Schaff & Wace, cited above, p 1.
20. The same,p 212f.
21. The letter is given in the work of Schaff & Wace cited above (n 2), Vol XIII, pp 38-42.
22. cf. St Thomas Aquinas, *Summa Theologiae*, II-II, q 128.
23. *The Dark Night*, Bk II, ch 20, n 2.
24. Romans 5:5
25. cf. Matthew 25:40
26. Council for Social Welfare, quoted in Combat Poverty Agency, *Fair Shares*, Dublin 1991, p 45.

CHAPTER FOUR

Entrapment and Release

Our life, like a bird, has escaped
from the snare of the fowler
Indeed the snare has been broken
and we have escaped.
Psalm 123

Trapped

I do not think anything feels worse than being trapped. A friend of mine tells me how he discovered an underwater cave while swimming. There was enough air in it for him to come up and sit on the rocks, admiring the effect of the sunlight from outside. But once, when he thought it was time to swim back out, he could not bring himself to enter the water again. His will to swim had vanished. It returned eventually, but for half an hour or so he was trapped – by the water, by the rocks and mainly by his own loss of courage.

Being trapped is something that everyone experiences in one way or another. One can be trapped in a situation of one's own making or in something that happens by accident. Marriages or other relationships, when they go wrong, a job or not having a job, being under physical attack, these are experiences of being trapped.

As a person's life unfolds, his or her movement towards God becomes an issue. Then the sense of being spiritually trapped is sure to be experienced. Not just the sense of being trapped in an anti-spiritual habit or system, being trapped by sin. But also being trapped by spirituality itself, by a prevailing religious climate, by previous ideas one is out-growing, or perhaps by a religious commitment that has been made. Whatever is there, whatever is fixed, whatever has been done already, whether it is good or bad, can come to present itself as a trap. There is no possibility of settling down at a point of spiritual growth as if it was something fixed and settled for all time. It is always necessary to move on and up. Yesterday's achievement can be today's trap.

Escape Attempts

A saving feature of entrapment is that it takes a long time to realise that we are trapped, so that hope is not snuffed out. We might not be able to see a way out, but we see some things we can try.

Even the person trapped in the underwater cave could see that, just by waiting, his paralysis of will might go and he could dive into the water quickly before it came back. The experience of being trapped is a deep education in self-knowledge. It is then that a person learns what his or her real weaknesses and strengths are, how the emotions respond, how cool the head is, what he can endure. Solving the problem of a difficult marriage will be a most important growth experience for the wife and husband, whether they regain their love for each other or find that it is irretrievably gone. Bringing a friendship to closure, or to new life, is another experience that can be a means of growth for people. At a deeper level still, the personal effort of meeting one's own fear or anger or sadness is a renewal for anyone, even if they cannot remedy the causes. It is a journey of self-discovery, even if it is not a successful attempt to escape.

The alternative to trying to escape is giving up, either by collapsing into inactivity or by launching into a frenzy of activity. When people give up, they do not escape, and they do not grow either, because of the way they switch off their mental powers. A kind of inertia takes over. It is sometimes called escapism, but it is really a way of *not* trying to escape, but only to forget. A person may, for instance, try various ways of stupifying himself, with drugs, say, or drink (though these might be things a person could consciously try too, even if unwisely, as part of a genuine attempt at escape). The biblical book of Qoheleth, or Ecclesiastes, tells of a person's attempts to find a way out of the futility of life. Reading it may help people to share the author's escape attempts without incurring the danger of trying everything themselves. But there is a world of difference between learning from real escape attempts, whether one's own or other peoples', and just giving up. In the latter case, there is neither escape nor growth, but in the former there is personal growth and there may be escape.

Banishment

All this may seem hopeless. I have deliberately refrained from claiming that spirituality will set anyone free from the snare they are trapped in. What I believe is that after all our escape attempts, whether they are successful or not, we still find ourselves dissatisfied. It is as if we escaped from a trap, only to find that we were banished on an island. Whether we escape or not only affects the nature and the size of the trap we are in. An unsuccessful escape attempt will enable us to grow personally in such a way as to live through our entrapped existence. A successful attempt will fit us to live through our banishment. The essential human journey is the interior one that leads towards confronting one's issues in a personal way. So even if Ken, whom we met in Chapter One, escapes somehow from the unemployment trap, he will still be faced with making a go of life. The same holds for the other five people, and for everyone else as well. We are all exiles from the possibility of complete fulfilment. Not even spirituality can take away the pain of existence.

Banishment, though, is no more something to succumb to than a trap is. There is much for us to learn about ourselves, and for us to become, by trying to find our collective way out of exile. There are also collective and even global ways of giving in to banishment, like the poet's 'land of the lotus eaters.' The promises of 'good times now', that make the distribution and production systems work in modern western society, are a form of collective escapism paid for by the poorer populations of the world and the underclass of western society itself. Western life is little more than a global evasion of the issue. It is not a way of being human. The only way to be human is to embrace as equals everyone who is human, everyone in the family which Jesus Christ shows that we all belong to. The religious part of that is to refuse to believe in any god who is satisfied with less than full humanity from us. It is to insist on obtaining from God the power to be fully human. Recognising that God is our Creator, that we exist for him, and that it is only in union with him that we can be fully human, is what Ignatius of Loyola calls the Principle and Foundation (of spiritual growth.)[1] It is the essential first step in spiritual growth.

The Last Trap

The ultimate trap in which people find themselves, even assuming that they have found ways of dealing with impossible relationships and with addictions, is that of combining the acceptance of all human beings as members of the same family with remaining free and enjoying interior peace. Even accepting the people we actually have contact with, without letting the effort grind us down, can be so difficult that it feels like a trap. It is into the scenario of human beings trapped like this, and being honest enough to admit it, that God comes. He comes with teaching. He comes with example. Above all he comes with grace to form mankind into one great people of his own. God comes to work alongside his fellow men and women at the task of creating a new earth, which in due course will give way to a new and eternal heaven. In the crucified outcast, Jesus of Nazareth, God has begun the process of disentanglement. It is a process that will, no doubt, last as long as the world does. But it began, and is always recommencing, with individual people admitting to themselves what they feel, and then speaking plainly to one another about what is happening and how they see things.

The decisive move in people disentangling themselves from the last trap is expressed by Jesus in a word we usually translate 'repent.' What it really means is 'change your hearts.' In other words, the call of God is not in the first place a call to keep such and such commandments, not even the commandment of love itself. Rather it is a call to return to our true selves, our hearts. The honesty and truthfulness which I believe are the core of spirituality are simply this attentiveness to the heart, this discovery of our own conscience. The ongoing disentanglement of people's individual and social lives is the process of people listening to themselves and to each other.

Listening to what is most human in ourselves is a way of listening to the voice of Christ, who in the gospel identifies himself with every human person, even the least. The words of Christ himself, communicated by the teaching church, are meant to help us listen to our own hearts and express what we feel there. The Spirit of God gives added depth and sensitivity to our hearts. He enables people to recognise that it is not only the heart of human beings that is revealing itself, but also the heart of God himself. Disentanglement is perhaps the best word to express what is happening when we escape from the last trap. When a tangle is unravelled, the line is not cut or damaged in any way. It is not even improved. It is just restored to its right state. And as people disentangle their lives, they repeat one simple move over and over again, that of listening to their own and one another's hearts.

Rehabilitation

There is quite a sense of achievement in disentangling a fishing line or a rope. Still, even when the line is safely reeled up, there is room for anxiety that what happened before can happen again. Hearts that once before stopped listening to each other or themselves can stop listening again. It's not like getting out of a trap which can be destroyed, because the 'trap' is human nature itself. So it is vital that the disentanglement carried out by human hearts, in response to Christ's call to newness of heart, should be followed up with some kind of 'rehabilitation' – something like what people coming out of hospital or prison receive. Like the disentanglement itself, this occurs on three levels – teaching, modelling and empowering, that is, the teaching of Christ and of those who teach in his name, the modelling of Christ and of those who are taking him as their model, and the grace of Christ. Accepting Jesus Christ as one's own personal saviour is what St Ignatius Loyola calls entering the service of Christ the Eternal King.[2] After recognising God as one's personal Lord, the acceptance of Christ as one's mentor, guide and hero is the second great step forward in spirituality.

The teaching of Christ is basically the twofold commandment of love of God and of neighbour, often expanded with his other sayings, his parables and the Old Testament commandments of Moses which Christ makes his own. This commandment grows from the revelation of God's own love, shown above all in his becoming a human being, and in the relation of Father, Son and Spirit in God's own interior life. Learning this teaching, contemplating it and trying to understand it, provides the theoretical basis of our rehabilitation.

In addition to the teaching which Jesus gives, he is himself, in his own person, the great model or icon of what a restored human being is like. This applies not so much to his miracles and extraordinary qualities, which are mostly unique to him. What Jesus models for the human race is love for his Father, love for people, availability, courage, hard work, patience, and above all the suffering and death which he shares with every other human being. Having Jesus Christ as a model to look at and think about, and also having many other people who live in his Spirit available to us, is an important aspect of the spiritual rehabilitation of the human race.

Even more important than having Christ as teacher and model, is having him as the one who empowers us. Christ empowers people by giving them the gifts of the Holy Spirit. By the power of the Holy Spirit, Christ enables people to receive his teaching and to follow his example, and even to do things and to teach things which he himself never actually did or taught, but which the same Spirit inspires. So, the lives of St Patrick and Blessed Edith Stein are different from that of Jesus Christ in almost every detail. For all that, they clearly belong to the same spirit. Those whom the Spirit of Christ inspires are not just a handful of people, a few in every generation or country. This empowerment is there for everybody without exception.

There are basically three ways in which Christ empowers people, namely, prayer, the sacraments and what is called 'merit.' Prayer consists in asking God for the gift of his Spirit, as for example the disciples did in the Upper Room before Pentecost. People all over the world are still doing that every day, with no less striking results. The sacraments are religious rituals instituted by Jesus Christ himself. Baptism and the eucharist are the most important ones. In them, the Holy Spirit is quite literally bestowed on people who are disposed to receive him. By means of the sacraments, a person comes into direct physical contact with people who continue the line of those whom Jesus Christ himself sent out – and not just clergy either, but the wife or the husband whom a person marries, and indeed every person who is baptised. Merit, which is the third way in which the Holy Spirit empowers people, is the reward God gives to a person who allows himself to be empowered by him. For example, a person who cooperates with God's grace by practising honesty, is rewarded by God with a fresh and perhaps greater grace of honesty on subsequent occasions, like the people in the parable who, because they were faithful in little, were rewarded with much. Experience shows that this is one of the most important ways God makes his power grow in people.

Asceticism

The person who told me about his experience in the underwater cave, said that he suffered from loss of courage. Something like that endangers all our efforts to escape from traps, or to deal with addictions. The processes of disentanglement and rehabilitation depend a lot on will power. This is why the Church's annual Lent and Easter season of renewal begins with forty days of self-denial. It is the same in other religions, for example the Islamic Ramadan. While there is no longer, at least generally throughout the Catholic Church, a set of strict rules laying down how people are to deny themselves, nevertheless the clear invitation is there for everyone. Moreover, experience shows that it is impossible to make any spiritual progress, especially by way of disentanglement and rehabilitation, without a good deal of self-denial.

In this respect too, Jesus Christ is our model. He fasted for forty days before going to receive John's baptism at the start of his preaching ministry – that probably means that he did not eat between sunrise and sunset, as the practice then was, and as Moslems still do during Ramadan. He also on occasion rose very early, and sometimes did not go to bed at all, in order to pray – this is the origin of the practice of vigils. But the most fundamental form of his self-denial was accepting patiently what came his way, both the fatigue and difficulty of his work and the persecution that overtook him at the end of his life. His self-denial did not, however, prevent him celebrating at feasts and weddings, and relaxing when he needed to.

What we see in the life of Jesus are two sides of asceticism – the word comes from the Greek word for training, as in athletics. There is the active side and the passive side. St John of the Cross writes of the active and passive 'entry into the night of the senses'. The former is a deliberate and self-induced privation of things that give sensory enjoyment. In his rather stark way of writing, he advises:

> Endeavour to be inclined always:
> not to the easiest, but to the most difficult;
> not to the most delightful, but to the harshest;
> not to the most gratifying, but to the less pleasant;
> not to what means rest for you, but to hard work;
> not to the consoling, but to the unconsoling;
> not to the most, but to the least;
> not to the highest and most precious,
>   but to the lowest and most despised;
> not to wanting something, but to wanting nothing;
> do not go about looking for the best of temporal things,
>   but the worst,
> and desire to enter for Christ into complete nudity,
>   emptiness,
> and poverty in everything in the world.[3]

In passive purification, it is really God himself who is purifying us, by the things that he permits to happen, for example misfortunes or annoyances from outside, and, within ourselves, temptations and lack of consolation in prayer.

Something like both active and passive purification could occur in the case of a person who had no interest in growing closer to God. But when people engage in them as part of an effort to grow spiritually, there is explicit attention to God. A person either does them for the sake of God or accepts them from God's hands. By means of these purifications a person can cut through the layer of sensuality that prevents the heart from being spiritually alert.

There are two recent movements in psychotherapy that provide a human or scientific framework for the practice of asceticism. One is called *psychosynthesis*. It was developed by an Italian medical doctor called Roberto Assagioli. The other is linked particularly with an American psychiatrist named Gerald May, and grows out of the treatment of people who are suffering from addictions like alcoholism.

The core of Assagioli's theory consists in 'disidentification' and 'identification.' These mean detachment from things that are not oneself and discovery of the true self. For example, people may discover that they have identified so much with some talent, such as intelligence or being good-looking, that they are leading a very limited life as a result. What is needed by someone in this position, which is very common, is to discover *all* the aspects of herself or himself, and yet not identify with any of them. This helps the person to discover their true, spiritual and free self, which they then affirm by acts of the will, especially difficult ones. Among the methods used to discover and affirm one's true self are *visualisation*, and *interior dialogue*.[4] People can develop to a surprising extent by realistic visualisation of themselves in significant situations, say, being questioned by the police. Likewise by holding imaginary dialogues, with an enemy, perhaps, or a personal hero. A considerable number of familiar spiritual practices turn out to have a basis in Assagioli's theory.

May's theory[5] too, although like Assagioli he is a medical doctor, resembles theology almost as much as medicine. The basic fact , for him, is that God alone can satisfy the human person. Anything other than God (including practices of religion) can become the object of an addiction. Any addiction is harmful to the personality – whether it is a positive addiction (attachment), or a negative addiction (aversion.) Some people are positively addicted to alcohol, and others negatively, but both addictions are harmful. So addictions need to be broken, and the crucial question is how to do so. The obvious way is to substitute one addiction for another, say, over-eating instead of over-drinking. Substitution can be helpful, but care is needed in the choice of substitute addictions. They can stunt the personality like any addiction. The only really good way to deal with an addiction is to accept the void of the unsatisfied appetite, to stay with it long enough to discover that it is really a kind of spaciousness and freedom, not a void, and that in this freedom we discover our true selves and God. Grace makes a crucial contribution to this addiction-breaking process.[6]

Asceticism, as I mentioned earlier, runs counter to the sensuality which contemporary marketing practices cultivate, and so it is almost a subversive act. But it has even more significance than that, socially speaking, because it contributes to the bonding of society. The large and growing underclass in modern western society is characterised by great and even extreme privation. This is even more true of the global underclass. People who practice asceticism not only help God to change their lives. They also help impoverished people to appreciate the hidden benefits of their condition, and help to reduce the pressures of envy and self-pity. By promoting social and global solidarity, asceticism makes an important contribution to achieving the goals of Christian gentleness.

Meeting Someone Free
Although people's own cooperation is necessary, it is God who distentangles them. God often does this by bringing them into contact with someone who is already free – not just someone caught in a different and more interesting trap, but someone really free. The life-stories of the saints usually tell how a meeting with someone else liberated them, and how meeting them in turn liberated others. Sometimes it is no more than a meeting, out of which comes the conclusion, 'Well, if she (or he) can be like that, so can I.' Sometimes it is a long-term friendship or even discipleship, with one person serving a kind of apprenticeship in freedom to another. Behind these encounters and relationships, there is the much more fundamental encounter with God. God alone is really free, and can make people free. At times, this direct relationship with God is the only relationship involved in a person's becoming free. The well-known story of the conversion of St Antony of Egypt is such a case. Anthony had inherited great wealth, but when as a young man he entered a church where the gospel words, 'Go sell what you have, and give to the poor,' were being read out, he immediately knew that there was nothing for him in life except to divest himself of his property and take up prayer and the service of God. He retired to a remote place, where he was greatly loved by the local people, and eventually attracted many disciples. He became one of the principal originators of the monastic movement, and thus had great influence on the history of Europe, due entirely to his response to a direct call from God.

Something similar occurred at the decisive moment of St Augustine's conversion. He found it impossible to restrain his sexual desires, though conversations with several people had given him a great longing to break away from his unchaste life. It was not, however, in one of these conversations that the decisive moment came. It came when he was alone and heard a child's voice singing nearby 'Take up and read! Take up and read!' (as in some kind of game.) He picked up a copy of St Paul's Letters that was at hand, opened it and through his tears 'read silently,' as he tells us, 'the first portion of scripture on which my eyes lighted: "Not in revelling and drunkenness, nor in debauchery and licentiousness, not in quarrelling and jealousy. But put on the Lord Jesus Christ, and make no provision for the flesh, to gratify its desires."' With that, 'a light of certainty turned on in my heart, and all the fog of doubt disappeared.'[7] The direct action of God's grace is always present in spiritual growth, even when there is also a relationship with one or more other people.

Whichever way spiritual awakening and growth takes place, it is always very beneficial or even necessary to receive pastoral care from someone who is really free, at least to some extent, and who has the skill and the grace to minister to one's new-found freedom in Christ. Seeing oneself reflected in the responses and presence of the other person is an important aid to owning one's own freedom. Even someone as independent-minded as St Paul eventually sought out those who were apostles before him, so as to make sure he was not mistaken about his own grace: three years after his conversion he went to Peter, and many years later, to a group of the 'recognised leaders' of the Church.[8] Freedom is something that is 'caught' from someone else. It cannot exist at all unless it is 'caught' from Christ himself. A purely human 'freedom' invariably turns out to be an addiction or an enslavement of some kind in disguise.

God Alone

The point made by Gerald May, that only God is capable of satisfying our desires, deserves further consideration at this point. It may seem quite shocking. Various objections to it arise. For one thing, is it not at an advanced stage of spirituality, rather than the initial 'disentanglement' stage, that we can expect to be satisfied with God alone? For another, why would we human beings be in this world, with all its enjoyments, if our real object of enjoyment was supposed to be God? And, most fundamentally, how can we enjoy God anyway? These are all important questions.

It is certainly surprising, but experience of the spiritual life shows people being very attached to God as soon as they begin their process of disentanglement, then afterwards being or seeming to be less religious, and finally finding themselves becoming more absorbed in God again (if, that is, they persevered through the second phase). These stages all belong to the beginning of the spiritual life. But not even the third of these steps contains as much religious excitement, so to speak, as the very first stage. The 'first fervour' of people at any age when they start taking spirituality seriously is a well-known phenomenon. It is not by any means to be despised. Important things happen to a person during his stage of initial enthusiasm for the things of God. People need to be supported (even put up with) and listened to during that stage. It is necessary to help them not to get disillusioned when it begins, as it were, to wear off. And it is sometimes necessary to help them to admit their enthusiasm and not to be ashamed of it.

The 'latency' period, which follows the beginning of spiritual experience, can seem to involve an absence of God, and be felt as a regression. In fact it is nothing of the kind, but a deepening of one's sense of God as he really is. The third step of greater intimacy with God is much more like a dark night than the original encounter with God was. To a great extent, one has to walk by faith alone at this stage and afterwards. The important point to be aware of is that these developments, these steps forward, only come when a person has allowed himself or herself to experience the first stage. So, if people ignore excitement or religious feelings, what happens is that the start of their consciously lived spiritual life is delayed. Had they accepted these feelings when they came initially, then they would end in due course, and the people concerned would be ready to embark on the life of pure faith. It can be dangerous for a person to resist his initial religious awakening, because then he will be in a more vulnerable position when it comes and is taken away again later in life – for example, when he is trying to teach his children something about God, or even to minister as a priest.

Why does God give us so many things to enjoy in the world if it is really God we are meant to enjoy? That would certainly be a serious difficulty if it were a matter of 'either/or.' But experience shows that it is not a matter of 'either/or.' Everything has its place in human life, though the exact place of everything differs from one person's life to another's. It is God who gives people their sense of balance, making it known that even the best and most enjoyable things are gifts from him, while even the worst things are at least permitted by him, so that they cannot be utterly unbearable. At all stages of life, God makes himself available to people for what God is – creator and redeemer. Images or ideas of God need not be permanently satisfying. They are always growing and changing and having to be discarded. God is always communicating himself in new ways, and allowing everything else to emerge in fresh beauty.

How is it possible to enjoy God? Enjoying God is something to experience, rather than to talk or write about. It is a matter of staying with God, as you actually experience God, whether that is in a positive way, or in a negative way, or even in a dull, switched-off way. Stay with your actual experience of God, and enter into it. Meet the God who lies at the centre of the experience, as Moses did with the burning bush.[9] All that is required is a little faith, and a little steadiness of mind, to stay with the God you are experiencing. Nothing else is required, not even that you should be a good person. That can wait. God alone, as you actually experience God, is enough.

Patience

St Teresa of Avila (1515-1582) has a little poem usually known as her 'Bookmark' but entitled 'Efficacy of Patience' in the latest English edition of her work. [10] Here it is:

Let nothing disturb thee,
Let nothing dismay thee,
All things pass,
God never changes.
Patience attains
All that it strives for.
He who has God
Finds he lacks nothing.
God alone suffices. [11]

Patience attains all that it asks for. Or, as the more homely English proverb has it, everything comes to him who waits. Waiting, or patience, is not fatalism. It is not doing nothing, and it is not frenzied activity. What patience is meant to be is an ingredient of every action, mental or physical, and it is, I think, the very thing that prevents any action being frenzied. There is a traditional Irish story that illustrates very memorably the power of patience, entitled *Briseann an Fhoidhne ar an gCinniúint* ('Patience Overcomes Destiny') and I discovered from the way people in Africa responded to it that it can cross a cultural divide. The story goes like this:

A woman was a long time waiting for her first son to be born. And when he was, a spirit came to the woman and told her, 'On his twenty-second birthday, he will die.' The prophecy made her very sad when she heard it, but she soon forgot her sorrow as she nursed and washed and dressed her son. With the passing years, she grew ever more fond of the boy, who was very good-tempered, and playful and healthy. In due course he went to school, where all the teachers were charmed with him, and he was much in demand for his ability at music and sport. He did even better when

he went to secondary school, and eventually won a scholarship to university. There he completed an honours degree
and returned home to celebrate his twenty-second birthday.
He was amazed to find his mother in tears when he arrived,
and it was only then that she told him what the spirit said
when he was born. 'Go up to your room,' his mother said, 'at
twelve o'clock tonight, and stay there away from everyone,
with the door and the window locked.' He did so, sitting on
a chair in the middle of the room. Then, at midday, a creature like a small worm crawled up the outside wall and came
into the room through a crack in the window. It crossed the
floor and climbed the boy's leg and on to his arm, and all the
time he did not move. Finally it went up his neck and into
his hair, then down his forehead and in behind his glasses,
without him moving at all. Then the creature went down his
neck, dropped on to his knee, crawled down his leg to the
floor, crossed the floor again and went out the same crack as
he came in. The boy stayed where he was until midnight,
and then opened the door and ran down to tell his mother
that he was well. She was there with some old people who
were keeping her company, and when they heard what happened one of them said, '*Briseann an fhoidhne ar an gcinniúint.*'

The point of the fable is that inner strength, the ability to give
things the attention and the time they need, however much that
may be, achieves everything. Patience means that what we are
trying to do will have all of ourselves in it. If what we are trying to
do is something spiritual, that means we have opened ourselves
fully to the action of God in it. Endurance, according to St Thomas,
is the chief expression of courage,[12] and it is the chief expression
of charity according to St Paul.[13] It is one of the main ways in
which a human being can come to resemble God, who is eternal,
and who is completely present in all that God does. On the other
hand, impatience or haste spoils everything (it is really the result
of sensuality.) The line of the psalm rings very true, 'Be still, and
know that I am God' (Psalm 45:11).

Gethsemane
Asceticism, both active and passive, and patience, are important
parts of the disentanglement process. There is something else,
however, which I think is even more important. It can be explained
by means of the experience of Jesus in Gethsemane. Gethsemane
was a favourite spot on the Mount of Olives near Jerusalem where

Jesus used to go when he wanted to be on his own. After the Last Supper he went there, accompanied by his three closest disciples. When he reached the spot, as Matthew tells it, 'he began to feel sadness and anguish.'

> Then he said to them, 'My soul is sorrowful to the point of death. Wait here and stay awake with me.' And going on a little further, he fell on his face and prayed. 'My Father,' he said, 'if it is possible, let this cup pass me by. Nevertheless, let it be as you, not I would have it.' He came back to the disciples and found them sleeping, and he said to Peter, 'So you had not the strength to stay awake with me for one hour? Stay awake, and pray not to be put to the test. The spirit is willing enough, but human nature is weak.' Again, a second time, he went away and prayed: 'My Father,' he said, 'if this cup cannot pass by, but I must drink it, your will be done!' and he came back again and found them sleeping, their eyes were so heavy. Leaving them there, he went away again and prayed for the third time, repeating the same words. Then he came back to the disciples and said to them, 'You can sleep now and take your rest. Look, the hour has come when the Son of man is to be betrayed into the hands of sinners. Get up! Let us go! Look, my betrayer is not far away.'[14]

In the experience at Gethsemane, Jesus is far beyond either the self-discipline of the forty days in the desert or the patience of his three years of labour. And yet his arrest, condemnation, torture and crucifixion have not begun. He is at the stage when his heart awakened to the full realisation of what is happening to him. He is faced with the agonising choice of accepting or rejecting his destiny, and he can only resolve this struggle by means of anguished prayer. It is an experience of interior awakening, interior suffering and almost desperate pleading. In it, what is yet to come is confronted and accepted for what it is, a bitter cup of suffering and his Father's will. By this experience, Jesus prepares for his cruel, almost Auschwitz-like, destiny.

The Gethsemane experience of Jesus corresponds to something everyone has to go through: an interior awakening, a realisation of the awfulness of it all, a launching of oneself into the arms of God, and receiving the gift of his strength. I would see this kind of experience as the last or nearly-last stage of the beginning of a spiritual life, rather than anything more advanced. After it, a person is certainly leading a really spiritual life. Before it, a person has not had his or her interior baptism, so to speak. None of that should be taken to suggest that there will not be any more Gethse-

mane-type experiences for the rest of one's life – though I think
the first one could be the most decisive of all. The essential thing is
the profound reality of it. The anguish is real, so is the decision-
taking; the entrusting of oneself to God is also real, as is the courage and the strength that God gives.

A priest I know described the following as his own personal
Gethsemane experience. While he was in his last years in the seminary, coming up to ordination as a subdeacon (as it then was), he
woke up to the fact that the long years he had already spent away
from home preparing for the priesthood were only a taste of the
solitude that would be forever. He began to think how much better it would be to go back to his native place and rejoin his own
people. He even notified the authorities that he might not go on,
and in the event they took his warning seriously enough not to
order a Breviary (the prayer-book he would need to recite the
Divine Office) for him. He decided to give a day of a retreat the
seminary was making to praying about the issue, and he spent
hours walking through the leafy countryside reading Psalm 118:
'My part, I have resolved, O Lord, is to obey your word.' As he
prayed his way through the longest of the Psalms, he was overcome by a sense of absolute certainty that he should go on to be
ordained, and be sure that God would be with him. Afterwards,
as he looked back on that day, he was and is, he assured me, certain both of the reality of the experience, and of the fact that he
was much closer to the start of his spiritual growth than to anything like holiness.

Joy
The very beginnings of spiritual growth are often quite absorbing
and exciting, like the first communion day or confirmation day of
a child. But a thread of joy runs throughout the beginning stage,
alternating with bleakness or pain. This is the experience of consolation succeeding desolation that Ignatius of Loyola writes
about.[15] The desolation may actually occupy more time than the
consolation, but it is the consolation that is especially valuable
They are, as it were, the right and left hands of God, both convey-
ing something of God and leading us to him, and yet the joy con-
veying most of God's essential nature, and the desolation most
about ourselves and how far we are from him. With time, we
come to recognise in times of desolation how vulnerable we are,
how small we are. It brings out something of the pathos or tragedy
of life which consolation does not eliminate but rather responds
to. When we grow that far, I think we tend not to lose our heads in

joy, but not to be crushed by affliction either. It is as if our centre of gravity was shifting, perhaps unconsciously, to a sense of God's permanent loving presence to us, and of his presence as saviour to a bruised and suffering world. Temptations to the grosser sensual sins are not usually habitual at this stage, I think, though a sudden rush or shock of temptation may easily catch a person off guard. The standing temptation is more likely to be negligence, thinking that having got this far one is safe and so neglecting the ascetic and other practices that got one there. A person at this stage who does not allow himself or herself to get entrapped again, will have moments of real joy. But he or she can also be sure that the real work is only about to begin, leading to a deeper and more permanent joy.

Notes

1. *The Spiritual Exercises of St Ignatius*, trs L. Puhl SJ, Loyola University Press, Chicago 1951, p 12 (n 23).
2. The same, p 43ff (nn 91-100).
3. 'Ascent of Mount Carmel', in Kavanaugh & Rodriguez, *The Collected Works of St John of the Cross*, Institute of Cermelite Studies, Washington 1979, p 102f. Although the word 'not' occurs many times in the passage, the key word is 'endeavour'.
4. cf. Assagioli,R, *Psychosynthesis*, The Aquarian Press, Wellingborough, Northamptonshire 1990.
5. cf May, G, *Addiction & Grace*, Harper & Row, San Francisco 1988.
6. The role of grace in overcoming addictions is dealt with more fully in Chapter Seven.
7. *Confessions*, Book 8, ch 12.
8. Galatians, chs 1 & 2.
9. Exodus 3:1-6
10. cf. *The Collected Works of St Teresa of Avila*, Vol III, trs K. Kavanaugh and O. Rodriguez, Institute of Carmelite Studies, Washington DC, 1991, p 386.
11. E. Allison Peers (ed), *The Complete Works of St Teresa of Jesus*, Vol III, Sheed & Ward, London, 7th ed., 1972, p 288.
12. *Summa Theologiae*, II-II, q 123, art 6.
13. 1 Corinthians 13:4,7
14. Matthew 26:36-46
15. *The Spiritual Exercises of St Ignatius*, as above, pp 141-150, (nn 313-336).

CHAPTER FIVE

Growing in Union with God

How can I repay the Lord
for his goodness to me?
The cup of salvation I will raise,
I will call on the Lord's name.
Psalm 115

Gethsemane, the Beginning

In this chapter I will try to describe growing in union with God. By that I mean, growing in love of God. I intend staying as close to my own experience as in other chapters. I think this is something I or anyone can do. Anyone who has tried to remain with Christ during his passion, even if like the repentant thief on Calvary he or she is still very common clay, really does grow in union with God. This happens in a real, flesh and blood way, not in a way that is mysterious or unknowable. The only thing that people usually lack is the realisation of what is happening in their own experience. For everyone, union with God begins with accepting God's will as Jesus did in Gethsemane. It keeps on growing after that. This is the third crucial moment in spiritual growth.

The Gethsemane experience is that of being a child of God, and of being asked by God to drink a very bitter chalice, a chalice that contains the whole range of human suffering. It is more than an experience, it is a *choice* of accepting this bitter chalice, out of love for God, for people and for oneself. That choice, as it were, consecrates one's subsequent experience and conduct, no matter how imperfect a person one still is. Jesus was sinless entering his passion. The thief who repented was far from sinless entering his. But that thief's acceptance with Jesus of his fate brought him union with Jesus on earth and in heaven. My personal experience of living after the completest possible commitment to Christ has been one of considerable personal inadequacy, and I know that the experience of many others has not been much different. But the original acceptance with Jesus of the Father's will has produced a dynamic of growth over the course of life. It is a growth which, in its own way, as we shall see, follows the course of the passion, death and risen life of Jesus. Not just the course of his passion ending in his death, corresponding to our death, but also the course of the risen life of Jesus up to his ascension and beyond. In other words, great progress in union with God is not meant to be

76

complete only at death. It is meant to have gone a long way quite early in life. Amazingly, not only the path of Christ's suffering but also that of his death, and even his resurrection and risen life, are to be followed in everyone's life.

What I am here presenting corresponds to the last, or the two last, stages of spiritual living as traditionally described in the church. From early times, three stages are distinguished – that of beginners, that of those making progress and that of those who are perfect. Later writers refer to these stages as the purgative, illuminative and unitive ways. Other writers divide the last into two stages, corresponding to the passion and to the risen life of Jesus. This is the division followed by Ignatius of Loyola in his *Spiritual Exercises*: people of the Third Week (of the Exercises) are living with Jesus in his passion, those of the Fourth Week are living with him after his resurrection. I agree with a recent writer who complains about the inadequacy of the three-stage division to express the experience of people trying to live for God.[1] But what really matters is that the unitive way or the Third and Fourth Week experience is not abstract theory, but very definite experience. Often the only thing people need is a little help to realise what is happening.

Suffering with a Purpose

In its usual crisp way, the fifteenth-century work called *The Imitation of Christ* sums up the human situation: 'Even if you arrange everything to suit your own views and wishes, you will always find that you still have to suffer something, whether you want it or not, the cross will be always there.'[2] Suffering cannot be avoided, not only when things go wrong, but as the down side of things when they go right, and even as the cost of making things go right. Enormous effort is required for every major achievement, be it in sport, in music or in public life, or any other area. The effort required of Jesus of Nazareth to transform the spirit of his own people and ultimately of the whole world, brought him to conflict with the authorities and to death by crucifixion. That was the destiny or the vocation of Jesus. But the complete fulfilment of his vocation was accepting it in solidarity with the sufferings of everybody, and out of love for his Father. If suffering cannot be avoided, even in the case of Jesus Christ, is there anything that can be done about it? What can be done is to give it meaning and to endure it out of love. What we can do is to enlarge our vision. We can want the coming of God's kingdom enough to suffer anything for it.

It is not easy to enter this frame of mind. The cosy armchair or the public bar are not always conducive to it. Most often an experience like a retreat, or a pilgrimage to a place of special significance, or some other exceptional experience, is necessary to get someone to commit himself or herself to a project 'costing not less than everything.'[3] It may take a whole series of such experiences, spread over years, for a person to make the supreme sacrifice of wanting God's kingdom more than anything else. And at all stages, there remains the possibility of evading one's commitment and letting life pass by.

As well as people who deliberately set out on the path of suffering so as to enter into union with Christ, there are people who do not have the luxury of a choice about suffering: people caught up in political upheavals, people who are the victims of economic policies that require them to remain out of work or impoverished, people whose lives are shattered by droughts, volcanoes or tidal waves, people whose health breaks down. When the end of the road comes like this, the only freedom that remains is to look for an interior way of accepting it, or not to look for one. Gethsemane offers hope for people in these desperate situations. It invites the victim to the literally superhuman task of finding a loving and compassionate purpose behind the collapse of his or her world. This is a task which can only be accomplished in anguished prayer like that of Jesus in Gethsemane. I am not here advocating fatalism, and in a later chapter we will see how personal situations that seem hopeless can be turned around. But, as we will also see later, it is necessary in the end for people to face disaster humanly and with dignity. Helping people to do so is one of the greatest services of Christianity.

The key to Jesus's Gethsemane experience lies in the word 'Father'. It was the love which Jesus experienced between himself and God that led him to commit himself to the Father's will in Gethsemane. In the life of Jesus, love for God had a long history. It was born at home in Nazareth. It was nurtured in Jesus's relationships with people. A tender affection for human beings, and a tender affection for the God who loves people and who stays with them in their sufferings, are what enabled Jesus to accept the awfulness of what was about to happen to him in his passion. What mattered for Jesus was not, as seemingly it was for the leaders of the Irish Revolution, the symbolism and the glory of a blood sacrifice. For Jesus, what mattered was love for people and for God. No sacrifice was too great for that. Christ's readiness for superhuman endurance did not grow from any brutalising toughness. It grew from the seeds of very gentle human feelings.

Trial and Rejection

The whole first part of the passion of Jesus is about trial and rejection. He was delivered to armed servants of the religious authorities by one of his closest followers, who kissed him in order to identify him. Then the chief priests and the religious senate or Sanhedrin interrogated him. After that followed condemnation for blasphemy. To have him put to death, it was necessary to bring Jesus before the representative of the Roman authorities, Pontius Pilate. Pilate again interrogated him, sent him to Herod, had him scourged and then displayed him to the crowd to see what they wanted for him. Yielding to public demand, Pilate agreed to have Jesus crucified. And all this time the closest followers of Jesus were either nowhere to be found or denying that they ever had anything to do with him. Jesus underwent, in half a day, a crushing barrage of rejection.

But it did not crush him. Instead, Jesus responded in a very human and sometimes more than human way to those who rejected him. His Gethsemane experience had inspired him, so that his captors shrank back when they first came up to him. He spoke to them calmly and directly. To the follower who led the soldiers to him he said, 'Are you betraying the Son of Man with a kiss?' To the high priests and the Sanhedrin he answered plainly but with no denial of the greatness of his mission. To Pilate also he plainly stated the spiritual nature of his mission. Before Herod and the crowd he remained silent. There is an honesty and a directness of communication on the part of Jesus as he is passed from one authority to another, which express deep respect for all his enemies, even while refusing to yield to them. This attitude of Jesus led the Roman governor to write out the charge against him in words of secret admiration: 'Jesus of Nazareth, King of the Jews.'

Not all followers of Jesus who encounter trial and rejection do so because their good qualities are ignored. Very often, it is a grinding down of real defects of character that lies in store for whoever says, 'not my will but thine be done'. The authorities could present even Jesus himself as a dangerous subversive, but most of his followers have more obvious and more unlikeable things wrong with them. These are dealt with in searching and painful processes of trial and rejection, which the follower of Jesus can do nothing but accept. And, at the same time as the follower experiences the well-deserved correction of his character defects, he finds that, like Jesus, his good qualities are also being put to the test. The follower has to stand up for his 'not my will but thine be done' in a way which leaves him nowhere to hide. The ability to allow one's faults to be burnt off, and not to allow one's good qualities to be burnt off, over a long period, is an essential part of the final or unitive stage of spiritual living.

The crucial indicator that one is living through these trials at an advanced level is the capacity to show some measure of real love and respect for others in the course of the experience. Fierce anger might be a very natural response to a persecutor, but it does not indicate close union with God, in whom there is nothing of what we know as anger. Neither do a numb denial of what is going on, or a merely assumed courage, or sarcastic expressions of respect. Only real strength and real respect for one's opponents, whether their attitude is justified or unjustified, can be taken as a sign that a person is spiritually growing. This is because such an attitude can only come from the Spirit of God.

At the root of union with God is the desire to share Christ's work as saviour of the world, not in the first instance by doing this task or that, preaching or whatever, but simply by living one's life with the world's salvation in view. What that means is, using one's whole being to express the desire that God's kingdom may come. There is a deep priestliness in this attitude. It is more than appropriate for ordained priests, but it is not by any means confined to them. God wants absolutely everyone to unite themselves with his Son's work in this way.

Carrying the Cross

After trial and rejection Jesus had to accept his sentence. It began with carrying his own cross-beam to the place where upright stakes stood ready for condemned people. Any journey is very deeply symbolic in a human life – there is no turning back, old and familiar things are left behind. New and possibly terrible things are expected. Incidents occur on the way which are filled with significance. And in a strange way the traveller is always alone. But when the journey is to the place where the traveller knows he is going to be killed, the symbolism is not only deep but tragic. The journey of Jesus from the judgment-place to Calvary symbolises his whole life, from the annunciation to Mary at Nazareth to his sacrificial death. Carrying his cross-beam on the journey symbolises that his crucifixion was the goal of his whole life.

The last journey of Jesus was to a little hill called Calvary. This fact too is invested with the symbolic power of hills as places where God is met and worshipped: Mount Sinai, Mount Zion, Croagh Patrick. Externally, the journey of Jesus to Calvary was to fulfil a judicial decree of the Roman Empire, on the demand of the local religious authorities. Internally Jesus was accepting his fate as the task which his Father was asking of him for the salvation of the human race. It was a great religious event, a spiritual action at the core of human history. It merited all the blessings needed for human salvation and for the establishment of God's kingdom of justice, love and peace.[4]

The gospels only mention two incidents on the journey of Jesus to Calvary. (The traditional Way of the Cross at Jerusalem records many other incidents.). The two gospel incidents are particularly significant. First, there is the compelling of a man named Simon of Cyrene to carry the cross with Jesus. Apart from the physical relief this must have been to Jesus, Simon represents every person who associates himself or herself with Jesus in carrying the cross for the salvation of mankind. Simon symbolises the need Jesus has for co-redeemers. He shows that Jesus is not meant to carry out his task completely alone. St Paul catches this thought when he writes of completing in his own body what is wanting of the sufferings of Christ.[5] In the other incident, Jesus speaks to the women of Jerusalem who are commiserating with him. He tells them to weep not for him, but for themselves and their children. This directs attention away from the suffering of Jesus, on to the people for whose sake Jesus is undergoing all this suffering. It is not Jesus, but these women, and the whole human race they represent, who are in a pitiable state. The women and all their fellow human beings are invited to weep *with* Jesus for the human race, instead of weeping *for* him. And the powerfully calm way Jesus speaks to them marks him out as the active figure in what is taking place, not a helpless victim.

As the months and years of a life offered to God in union with Jesus unfold, incidents occur which have their own great significance. In every life these will be unique. It is important to keep track of them, as we will see later when we consider the means for growing spiritually. What the two incidents recorded on the journey of Jesus to Calvary say is that great personal openness is due to everyone one meets along the way, whether a Simon who helps or women who commiserate, and that those suffering in union with Jesus can rise above their sufferings and show them to the world as something not to be grieved over. Not only Jesus himself, but the repentant thief crucified beside Jesus, was able to rise above his personal suffering in this way. The carrying of the cross shows how to transform and overcome the sufferings of life .

Words from the Cross

On Calvary, Jesus was stripped of his remaining clothing and fixed to the cross. He was left hanging there in such a way that he could only breathe by pushing himself up on his nail-pierced feet. Other condemned people were hanging on their crosses near him. There were also some guards, some sight-seers and a little group of his followers, mainly women. The gospels show Jesus speaking several times during those last painful hours of his life. These words from the cross show what Jesus was feeling interiorly. They also show what the follower of Jesus may expect to feel as his or her life unfolds after accepting God's will.

The seven words from the cross are:

A. (In St Matthew's & St Mark's gospels)

1. 'Eli, eli, lamma sabacthani.' that is, 'My God, my God, why have you forsaken me.'[6]

B. (In St Luke's gospel)

2. 'Father, forgive them, they do not know what they are doing.'[7]

3. Then [one of the criminals hanging there] said, 'Jesus, remember me when you come into your kingdom.' He answered him, 'In truth I tell you, today you will be with me in paradise.'[8]

4. Jesus cried out in a loud voice saying, 'Father, into your hands I commit my spirit.' With these words he breathed his last.[9]

C. (In St John's gospel)

5. Seeing his mother and the disciple whom he loved standing near, Jesus said to his mother, 'Woman, this is your son.' Then to the disciple he said, 'This is your mother'. And from that hour the disciple took her to his home.[10]

6. After this, Jesus knew that everything had been completed and, so that the scripture should be completely fulfilled, he said: 'I am thirsty.'[11]

7. After Jesus had taken the wine [they held up in a soaked sponge to his mouth] he said, 'It is fulfilled,' and bowing his head he gave up his spirit.[12]

The seven words reveal the inner life of Jesus as he was stripped of his selfhood in death . The phase of a person's unfolding life of union with God that they represent is not necessarily the person's physical death, but the moment when one is deprived of all pride and selfhood in union with Christ. After this comes more life, emptied of all attachment to self and seeking only what God wants. The seven words do not relate to the last words of a person's physical life, so much as to the last words of one's self-filled and self-directed life, and one's acceptance of new life in God.

The only one of the words from the cross given by both Matthew and Mark is given in Aramaic (by Mark, while Matthew gives it in Hebrew). It comes close to transcribing the words actually uttered by Jesus. It consists of the opening words of Psalm 22, a psalm of lamentation in the midst of terrible suffering. They express an awful sense of being abandoned by God. Jesus did not have this sense at all times during his passion, but it was one of the things he experienced. It is also something experienced by everybody as part of a deepening union with God. It feels as if it is lasting for ever. But as Psalm 21 itself shows, the person who remains as faithful as he or she can to the God who seems to have abandoned them, experiences the reawakening of the sense of God's closeness:

> For he has never despised
> nor scorned the poverty of the poor,
> from him he has not hidden his face,
> but he heard the poor man when he cried.[13]

The same psalm is referred to in the sixth word, (from St John), 'I am thirsty:'

> Parched as burnt clay is my throat,
> my tongue cleaves to my jaws.[14]

On one level, John, by giving this word from the dying Jesus, directs his readers to the psalm of lamentation and abandonment which expresses so well what Jesus felt on the cross. But on the level of reading the crucifixion narrative as representing the experience of every person who tries to live in union with Christ, the words 'I am thirsty' may be understood of the desire to anaesthetise oneself in the face of a terrible experience. A recent writer has suggested that the sense of abandonment by God,[15] the seeming disintegration of religion, may be a modern form of the 'dark night of the soul', which John of the Cross describes as 'horrible and frightful to the spirit'.[16] The widespread use of consciousness-changing substances today may be, at its most fundamental level, a symptom of that dark night. What corresponds in our lives to the cries of Jesus, 'My God, my God why have you forsaken me?' and 'I am thirsty' may be the two sides of the same experience. They invite us to live that experience, rather than drug ourselves out of it.

Three of the words of Jesus on the cross concern other people who were present: his prayer for the forgivenness of his executioners, his telling the repentant thief that they would be together in paradise, and his entrusting to one another of his mother and the beloved disciple. I do not think that they should just be seen as ordinary human interactions. Even the words Jesus used point to much more. Saying that his executioners and their masters did not know what they were doing means that what was really happening on Calvary was more than they could understand, although condemnations and executions were familiar exercises for them. What was really happening was a most profound mystery. But out of that mystery, as a response to the prayer of Jesus, comes forgivenness from the Father – forgivenness for those most at fault in the judicial murder Jesus was undergoing. This forgivenness is much more than generous human pardon, it is the deep enfolding of humanity in divine love.

The person united with Jesus in his passion is placed, and placed by God, on this level which is much deeper than any merely human interaction. At that level, a person is enabled to look with divine compassion on people in the midst of real wickedness, even when she or he is suffering the effects of the wickedness. This victim of wickedness is more concerned that his attackers should be responsive to divine mercy than that he should be spared. What is involved here is passing far beyond ordinary human responses of anger and revenge to something that is quite literally divine.

The repentant thief asked Jesus to remember him when he came into his kingdom. He seems to have understood more than Jesus did at that moment. The notice of condemnation over Jesus read, 'Jesus of Nazareth, King of the Jews'. But otherwise all the circumstances spoke of his rejection and powerlessness. The repentant thief had the intuition to know that Jesus really was a king. He can only barely have conceived the meaning of what he said to Jesus, but Jesus understood it, and responded gratefully: 'Today you will be with me in paradise.' Jesus accepts the repentant thief's sense of what is happening. He is comforted by it. He accepts the other man's equality with himself. All these thoughts and feelings must have been real at the human level, but they also went far beyond the human level. There was an expression of faith in the divine kingship of Jesus. That faith was joyfully accepted by the divine king. Jesus gave a promise of union with him in the divine home of paradise.

People who live in union with the crucified Jesus live both at the level of normal human feelings and at the level, perhaps only obscurely felt, of much greater realities taking place beneath the human ones. They are open to grounds of hope under the surface of terrible disasters. God himself accepts and confirms this faith, and points beyond present suffering to a joyful future.

The words that Jesus spoke to his mother and the disciple whom he loved, as they stood beside his cross, show human concern, the concern of Jesus that his mother should have someone to turn to after his death. But nothing in the passion of Jesus happens only at the human level. Everything in it is principally at the level of underlying divine realities. Jesus entrusts Mary and the beloved disciple to each other, for ever, in a relationship that is as permanent as his own relationship with Mary. No name is given for the beloved disciple in the gospel, even though he is generally taken to be John himself, the author of the gospel. It is beyond doubt that the beloved disciple of Jesus stands for every one of his disciples – even a last-minute convert like the repentant thief whom Jesus places beside himself in paradise. It is to every disciple without exception that Jesus entrusts Mary. It is a mark of true discipleship to receive her into one's house, that is, into one's intimate companionship. A deeply personal bond with the mother of Jesus is essential to Christian faith. It is as essential as praying for God's mercy on everyone, even one's enemies, and as being sure that there is a paradise of union with God waiting as the fulfilment of human life.

Union with Mary consists in sharing her devotion to her Son, in spite of the convulsive effect on her life-plans that this devotion involved for her: from ordinary marriage to virgin motherhood, and from virgin motherhood to standing beside a cross on Calvary. It consists also in chastity, whether at the level of virginity or at the level of married life, a chastity which may take long and patient struggles to attain. Union with Mary consists in a love of ordinariness or humility, and in a kindness that will make her as welcome a guest in one's own life as she was at the wedding in Cana. Devotion to Mary can vary widely in its expression – Bernard of Clairvaux and Vincent de Paul are quite different in their expressions of devotion to her. But a real devotion to her person, and to the core values of her life, is a mark of anyone who is intimately united with the crucified Jesus.

The remaining two words of Jesus on the cross are in strong contrast to the sense of abandonment by God and the bodily anguish of the first two we reflected on. In one, Jesus addresses his Father in a line from Psalm 30, 'Into your hands I commend my spirit',[17] and in the other, he draws the curtain on his passion and on his whole life, 'It is finished.' Both of these words express what

Jesus decided on in Gethsemane, when he accepted his Father's will in preference to his own. They express the way the spirit of Gethsemane holds together a life lived in union with the crucified Jesus. As well as that, the words 'It is finished' show that there is a definite turning point, a kind of spiritual dying, in the life of union. This is the fourth and last great moment in the spiritual life.

Dying

Dying is ceasing to be one of the human race, losing the selfhood one enjoyed and struggled in since birth. This loss of selfhood is not restricted to the moment of physical death, however. It is also what happens when a person's union with the crucified Jesus is consumated. There is then a sense of powerlessness, of being somehow an onlooker in one's own life, even though one continues to do all the things that have to be done as part of physical human life. But there is in addition a sense of being one with Christ, a Christ who is also without selfhood, and of waiting for whatever God will do next.

This kind of pre-death in Christ is one which elderly people or those broken in health often experience, though not all accept it for the spiritual reality it is, perhaps due to lack of anyone who can tell them what is happening. It is not necessarily a prelude to approaching physical death. It is the start of a stage of life in union with the resurrected Christ.

Resurrection

The resurrection phase of spiritual living follows a passion and death stage in union with Jesus Christ, in the course of which one may not feel or even be particularly holy. Jesus put on a par with his own passion the sufferings of somebody who, in his own eyes and the eyes of others, was justly condemned. The death-moment in a person's spiritual growth may come more or less unexpectedly, and it may pass unnoticed until it is reflected on. I do not think it would be right for me to give many details of what, as I look back, I can see as the dying phase of my life, except that it involved a series of rejections, condemnations and partings, which over a number of years I grew able to own and to live freely with. Most of them, I may add, were by no means undeserved. While they may not be all finished yet, the characteristic of the death-moment is that, after it, one cannot be crushed any more, whatever happens. This does not mean becoming impervious to pain. On the contrary, as the wounds which Jesus carried in his body tell us, the pain remains always, waiting to be tapped into or recalled.

What used to be called 'impassibility' (that is, being unable to feel pain) is not a characteristic of the resurrection-life of any human being, before physical death. I would be surprised if deep sorrow was not something that could be experienced by the risen Lord. We can be sure from experience that a death-and-resurrection experience in the course of a human spiritual life does not, by any means, put an end to suffering. It enables a person to suffer and to be there for others who are suffering in a way that is patient or peaceful, or at times, as in the case of some of the martyrs, even joyful. The terrible misery is taken out of suffering, as the sting is from death – but not the sorrow.

The resurrected person finds himself or herself again in Christ, but not necessarily in any position of prestige. The clearest symbol for the resurrected person is the utterly powerless person on the margins of society, though even people in prestigeous positions can know the marginality of the resurrected person when they take a stand for Christian and human values that are rejected by the powerful people in society – honesty, for example, or the sacredness of marriage, or the rights of the down-trodden. The mark of the resurrected person is to live fully in the power of the risen Christ, whether on the margins of society or not. It should be added, though, that people could believe in and support Christian or human values without having lived through Gethsemane and Calvary with Christ. That may show in the excess of human anger with which they meet opposition. The person who has suffered in union with Christ and risen with him will go about things with a considerable nobility and freedom of spirit. It is such people, when they have proved themselves, who come to be spoken of as saints.

They will, naturally, continue to live their normal human lives, whether as married people or people open to marriage or people committed to celibacy. They will do the shopping or go to work or collect their unemployment money just like everyone else. They could include the six people we met in Chapter One without any change in their circumstances. They will feel the cold and be left standing at bus-stops and lose their purses and be late for Mass, in the normal way. Where their holiness shows is in being available to the Spirit of God to reveal his action in the world, in small or big ways, often without their being conscious of it. Their effect on society will be as powerful and as unprogrammed as the appearances of the risen Christ to his disciples. A country or a city is Christian in proportion as its citizens have lived through from Gethsemane to Calvary in union with Christ and are available to

the Spirit of God all the time, even if that means being marginal-
ised by the powerful people in that society.

This kind of resurrected life which I am describing, mostly on
the basis of the anonymous experience of people who would generally count for very little, might look like a life confirmed in
grace. But I do not think this is so at all. A person who is living the
resurrected life on on the basis of union with Christ in his passion
can easily feel the attraction of reversing the course of his spiritual
life, and seeking the kind of very human vitality associated with
having or trying to get all kinds of wealth and enjoyment. People
can find the ordinary pleasures and comforts of resurrected life
dull by comparison with alternative possibilities. For this reason,
people living on the basis of their Gethsemane-Calvary experience need to maintain their commitment to the Father's will in
preference to their own. Sometimes this can be done just by considering how much value and fun there are in the simple things of
God and ordinary human life. But at other times a more determined effort may be required (a fast, a visit to Lough Derg, or a
holiday). There is, as the saying goes, no standing still in the spiritual life. One is nearly always rowing against the current.

Inspiring
Resurrection-life is not a steady and unwavering flow, but passes
through several stages. After the initial stage of availability for being moved by God's Spirit, there is a stage where a person speaks
or perhaps writes with deep inner authority, and inspires or even
commissions others to set out on a life of union with God. In his
own resurrection life, Jesus did both of these things, for example,
when he joined the two travellers on the road to Emmaus. It is,
perhaps, natural to assume that such actions are special to Jesus
himself as saviour of the world, but in fact very little in the life of
Jesus, even his resurrection-life, is completely special to himself.
The history of the church is largely the history of women and men
who found that they were able to speak of the things of God with
deep inner authority, and whose lives were based on the Gethsemane-Calvary experience of Christ, and whose authority was
recognised by the church. Some of them organised groups of followers into associations or movements, as did Brigid of Kildare,
Francis of Assisi, Ignatius Loyola, Nano Nagle, Catherine Mc
Cauley and many others. Others, like Thomas More, Damian of
Molokai and the Uganda Martyrs, simply said and did what they
believed in and inspired others by the example of their lives.
Many people have exercised authority and given inspiration like

this in very hidden ways, as parents, teachers, priests or even near-nobodies away from the beaten track of history. Many are still doing it. Their very anonymity is often a strength, as it makes them much harder to silence or to stop. The essential thing about all of them is that they have been set free by their meeting with Jesus Christ, and have entered and remained in his Gethsemane to Calvary experience. I doubt that anyone lives that experience and does not come out with the capacity to speak authoritatively and to inspire, but I am quite sure that no one should set out to speak authoritatively or to inspire who is not committed to living the death-and-resurrection experience of Jesus Christ.

Ascending and Sending
Advancing years usually make it necessary for resurrection-living people to move away from active ministry in public. Not infrequently even quite young people experience a call from the Spirit of God to a life not just on the margins of society but right outside it. This is the last and, in that sense, the highest stage of resurrection-life. In it a person directs his or her whole attention towards God and makes intercession for the world. Naturally, those who are called to live in this way still have their normal physical lives to lead, both individually and socially, so that they do many other things besides contemplation and intercession, but everything else is for the sake of those activities. Sometimes they live in monastic communities or as solitaries, sometimes they live 'just next door.' Their lives are not usually filled with consolation or delight any more than other people's, but only with a deep background sense of God's presence and God's love and God's attention to the world. The life they live is one of union with Christ 'always living to make intercession'[18] with the Father, and it is based on the lived Gethsemane-to-Calvary experience. Because the sending of the Holy Spirit is in response to the heavenly prayer of Christ and of the church on earth united with him, the mission of these people in the world is to obtain the blessings of the Holy Spirit for themselves and for others by their prayers. St Thérèse of Lisieux is among the best-known of those who have lived this stage of resurrection-life, but so may those who participate in the Jesuit-led Apostleship of Prayer. Almost everyone engaged in the active ministry in the church is conscious of how much they depend on the intercession of these special people, and of the saints in heaven whom they pass over to join. 'I will spend my heaven,' said Thérèse, 'doing good on earth.'[19]

Liturgy

Liturgy means, literally, the work of the people of God. The liturgy
of the church consists in the eucharist, the sacraments and the
Divine Office. Together they constitute a 'work' on the same level
as the witnessing, inspiring, contemplating and interceding that I
wrote about in the two preceding sections. This work is so important that it has been made a matter of 'obligation' by the Church –
it is obligatory to attend Sunday Mass, to go to confession and
communion at Easter, and (for deacons and other ministers, and
for religious) to recite the Divine Office. An unfortunate side-
effect of being made obligatory is that liturgy can seem like a bur-
densome duty. In reality liturgical activities are natural for people
living the resurrection-life based on the Gethsemane-to-Calvary
experience of Jesus . When people are trying to enter into the experience of the eucharist or of the sacrament of reconciliation with
very little commitment to living in union with the dying-and-
rising Christ, they are trying to move too far too fast. So it is very
important in places where a high degree of the practice of Christianity is the norm, for people to have a deep spirituality. It is even
more important for people who play key roles in Christian liturgy
to aim at deep union with Christ in his paschal mystery, that is,
his dying and rising from the dead. Failure to do so does not rob
the liturgy of all its meaning, but it does bring it perilously close
to hollowness and hypocrisy.

I think that there is no figure in the scripture who offers greater
comfort to those trying to follow Jesus than the repentant thief
who was crucified alongside him. The length of time he lived in
explicit union with Christ was not great, but he received the assurance that his union with Jesus would be very intimate. His sufferings were, so far as we can judge, well-merited. But that did not
make them unworthy of being associated with the undeserved
sufferings of Jesus, because he knew how to honour the goodness
he saw in Jesus. No matter how a person has lived, or is living, he
or she is 'not far from the kingdom of God.'[20] The start of union
with Christ is only a prayer away, and its growth is one step at a
time after that.

Notes

1. In *The Path to No-Self*, State University of New York, Albany,
NY 1991, Bernadette Roberts laments the failure of mystical writers to go beyond the 'honeymoon stage': 'It is assumed that after

transforming union and spiritual marriage there is no further
change or transformation and thus, there is nothing more to be
said ... [N]o one says anything about the time after the honeymoon, when life settles down to the nitty-gritty of ordinary living.
The failure to say anything about settling into a more mature
stage leaves the false impression that the unitive life ... is one con-
tinuous honeymoon' (p119). What I am doing here is presenting
the entire unitive life as a re-living of the post-Gethsemane experience of Christ.

2. *The Imitation of Christ*, trs Betty I. Knott, Collins, Glasgow 1963,
Bk 2, ch 12, p 104.

3. cf. T.S. Eliot, *Four Quartets*, 'Little Gidding', V, Faber & Faber,
London 1975.

4. The Preface of the Mass for Christ the King.

5. Colossians 1:24

6. Matthew 27:46 & Mark 15:34

7. Luke 23:34

8. Luke 23:42,43

9. Luke 23:46

10. John 19:26,27

11. John 19:28

12. John 19:30

13. Psalm 21:25

14. Psalm 21:16

15. 'In the anthropocentric twentieth century the same 'impasse'
or crisis point [that is, the dark night] may be experienced primar-
ily as a challenge to belief in a loving Lord; we discover, painfully,
that the deity we believed in when we started out on the road to
prayer quite literally does not exist, and that the divine reality
(whatever it may be) transcends all we had imagined.' S.Payne,
'The Dark Night of St John of the Cross: Four Centuries Later', *Review for Religious*,1990, p 891.

16. The Dark Night, ch 8, par 2. (Kavanaugh & Rodriguez, trs, *The
Collected Works of St John of the Cross* , p 312).

17. Psalm 30:6

18. Hebrews 7:25

19. Quoted in Jamart, *Complete Spiritual Doctrine of St Thérèse of
Lisieux*, Alba House, N.Y. 1961, p 105.

20. Mark 12:34

CHAPTER SIX

Ways and Means

If you trust in the Lord and do good
then you will live in the land and be secure.
If you find your delight in the Lord
he will grant your heart's desire.
Psalm 36

Introduction

What level of commitment does spiritual living require? Will an easy-going approach do, or does spiritual living need something like the commitment of the athlete? St Paul opts for the athlete's commitment:

> Do you not realise that, though all the runners in the stadium take part in the race, only one of them gets the prize? Run like that – to win. Every athlete concentrates completely on training, and this to win a wreath that will wither, whereas ours will never wither. So that is how I run, not without a clear goal; and how I box, not wasting blows on air. I punish my body and bring it under control, to avoid any risk that, having acted as herald for others, I myself may be disqualified.[1]

Growing in union with God is a challenging programme for a human being. At all stages, living spiritually is difficult. That much is evident from chapters four and five, and the programme of spirituality described in chapter seven is more demanding still.

The great difficulty of spiritual living is offset by the communal nature of Christianity. Christianity is church, a fact whose implications we will look at later in this chapter. It is world, national, regional and local churches, down to the 'domestic church'[2] of the family. Ways and means for spiritual living are worked out and implemented within the church. They are not uniform world-wide, but are adapted to people and places as the church itself is. It is not up to any particular person to say how everyone should live spiritually in everyday life. The individual people who are going to live spirituality decide that, in communion with each other and with their divinely appointed [3] leaders.

The 'ways and means' I offer here are things that have have been helpful to me in my efforts to live spiritually. They are indicators of the fact that everyone must find a practical programme for the liberating task of growing in union with God. That, I like to think, is what St Paul meant when he repeatedly wrote to his Christians, 'be imitators of me.'[4] Most of the things I suggest will probably be found helpful or necessary by many people, but there is no substitute for people discovering exactly what suits themselves in relation to God. My regret regarding this chapter is that, for reasons of space, I mostly have to express myself rather impersonally.

The points that follow are arranged in natural order, from the discovery of self to the discovery of God, and then to involvement in work for others.

Knowing, and Being, Oneself.

It is contact with the gospel that gives people their basic sense of who and what they really are. The gospel call to conversion is the clearest revelation of self. When people heard John the Baptist's call to repent, they immediately discovered themselves and asked, 'What shall we do?'[5] When Jesus had his long conversation with the woman at the well, her deepest impression was of someone who 'told me everything that I have done.'[6] When Peter preached on the first Pentecost, his hearers 'were cut to the heart' and asked what they should do.[7] James compares a person who listens to the word to someone 'who looks at his own features in a mirror', and the one who does not keep the word to someone who forgets what he looks like.[8] The shock of self-discovery on hearing oneself addressed by the word of God is as fresh and as powerful today as ever it was. Hearing the word of God read and preached in church, and reading it privately, have to be given first place as means of self-discovery.

The practice of people correcting each other is a well-tried means of self-discovery. It is very widely used today. Training programmes and programmes of personal development usually include what is called 'evaluation' by staff and peers. Families and other communities also have ways for the members to communicate their perceptions of each other, often informal ways. The dynamics of these systems of self-discovery require delicate management, so that St Paul warns parents (and everyone in charge of others) not to drive their charges to resentment.[9] Resistance to discovering what one is like is extremely strong in most people. A person who can correct others without making them feel judged is a very valuable member of society.

The present time has seen the development of several psychological systems of self-discovery, notably the Enneagram and the Myers-Briggs [Personality]Type Indicator. These have replaced a

very ancient but in its time quite useful division of human personality types into four: phlegmatic, melancholic, choleric and san-
guine. All of these systems have their uses, their dangers and their
potential for fun. But the primary means of self-discovery are observing how one is struck by the word of God and listening to
one's friends.[10]

It is when a person is trying to be true to himself or herself that
he or she is most alone, and it has to be like that. Being true to oneself involves not being controlled by other people and taking responsibility for who one is and what one does. It is when people
are alone like this, that they can be most conscious of the loving
presence of God.

Family Life

The only completely acceptable setting for a person to develop, is
the two-parent family. Even in that setting growing up is difficult,
and sometimes extremely difficult. But in any other setting, children are deprived of the possibility of a level of care which they
have every right to receive. It is certainly true that widowed parents often provide excellent parenting – John of the Cross was
brought up by his widowed mother – and that other single parents can sometimes provide a very good upbringing. But, to quote
a recent comment, 'there is significant coincidence between one-
parent families and many forms of disadvantage and deprivation.'[11] Family life is crucial, not just for social stability and psychological health, but also for spiritual living. It is there that the
essential spiritual relationships of fatherhood, motherhood and
childhood are experienced. It is there if anywhere that a child experiences love. These experiences are the most important things
to bring to growth in union with the God of love. Hence the *spiritual* importance of laws and customs that support married couples
and children in their family life, closely related to which are customs and laws that foster healthy sexuality in society. When these
structures break down, the spiritual life of society is likely to
break down too. Then people are faced with a heart-breaking task
of personal and social reconstruction. Such reconstruction may
have to be along the lines of the extremely difficult programme
described in Chapter Seven.

On the positive side, there is no human reality that can contrib-
ute more to union with God than the Christian family of husband
and wife, loving and respecting one another and loving and being
loved by their children. The four stages of the spiritual life, disentanglement, attachment to Christ, suffering with Christ and dying

and rising with him, can be lived out by families better, perhaps, than by any other group.

It is in the family that any person receives his or her childhood sense of worth and identity. And the usual place for the living out of an adult spiritual life is as husband or wife in a family. When a person is called by God to celibacy, there needs to be something that can only be compared to a marriage-relationship with God. Even then, while there is, for some people, a genuinely solitary way of living, celibates normally prefer to live with others in community.

Friendship

People often tell me that in their prayers they experience God as present, listening and friendly. They particularly value the fact that they can speak to God in a simple natural way, and do not need to have any secrets from God. What the bible says of Moses, that he spoke with God as a man speaks with his friend,[12] is what many people experience in their own lives. This is, I think, something which is available for everybody if they desire it. The *Imitation of Christ* encourages everyone to desire that kind of intimacy with God:

> The Children of Israel once said to Moses: 'Do thou tell us the message; we are ready to obey thee. Do not let us hear the Lord speaking; it will cost us our lives.' O Lord, my prayer is not like theirs, but with humble longing I pray with the prophet Samuel: 'Speak on, Lord; thy servant is listening.' I do not want to hear Moses speaking, or any of the prophets – Lord God, speak to me yourself. You inspired and enlightened the prophets, and you alone without them can teach us perfectly.[13]

Since this kind of friendship with God is available to everyone, it must certainly hold pride of place among a person's friendships.

But friendships with men and women are also of great value for personal growth and for spiritual living, not to mention for having any enjoyment in life. The word 'friendship' covers many different kinds of relationship, from being kind towards everybody, to 'best friend'. When it is said that people need friends in order to be fully themselves, and to grow spiritually, what is meant is that people need some others with whom they can be completely at their ease and in whom they can confide. Adolescence and youth are the times when friendships are at their most intense – 'pals' and boyfriends or girlfriends. But the need for

friends lasts throughout life. Jesus himself had close friends in the
two sisters Mary and Martha, and their brother Lazarus, who
lived at Bethany near Jerusalem.

I am not altogether sure whether there is an absolute need for
people who are living spiritually to have what are technically
called 'spiritual friendships'. What they do need are people in
whom they can confide concerning spiritual issues. But these
need not be friends in the sense of close friends: the relationship
could (and often should) be ministerial or professional rather than
purely personal. A spiritual friendship, in the strict sense, is one
that is bonded mainly by spirituality. Certainly there have been
and are many examples of such friendships, often between men
and women, and they can be very beneficial. The friendships between Basil and Gregory, Francis and Clare, Ignatius of Loyola
and his companions, Vincent de Paul and Louise de Marillac, are
among the best known. Many other people testify to the value
which such friendships have had in their lives. It is all to do, I
think, with the extraordinary freedom to be oneself which there is
in a friendship. This freedom stems from the fact that the friends
have no claim on each other except friendship – no financial claims,
no sexual claims, no professional claims. But the very freedom
that is at the heart of friendship means, I would suggest, that the
person who is living spiritually needs the freedom not to have
any intimate spiritual friend except God.

Memories

People's lives of union with God depend almost entirely on their
memories of God's action in their lives. Without these memories,
God seems remote, like a high government official or somebody
famous. God comes alive for someone when God is noticed taking
a part in his or her life. For many people, it is their memories of a
sacramental celebration like first communion or confirmation or
confession that fix their sense of a loving God. For others it might
be memories of prayer being answered or of coming to terms with
its not being answered. The net of memory can be thrown wider
to include all the experiences of childhood or youth, from the happiness of home life to its misery, from the terror of being a refugee
to the relief of arriving somewhere safe. Memory can also be
focused on the experiences of a day or a week just past, in what is
sometimes called 'an examination of consciousness.'

Cultivating personal memories is important to correct the
constant tendency to let life drift by unexamined, and the even

stronger tendency to direct attention away from experiences that are painful or threatening. People, for instance, who are very ashamed of some moral weakness can easily forget about it altogether. But when people make the effort to remember their experiences, they can discover how the good things that happen outweigh the bad things, and how even the worst things can be put right or coped with. People who neglect their memories allow unacknowledged experiences to pile up in their subconscious mind, with the good ones not being utilised for their beneficial power, and the bad ones causing disturbance.

A good practice is to read a gospel passage and afterwards to let your memory range freely. The memories, joyful or painful, that come up can then be prayed about. They can be shared with the Lord, and perhaps also shared with other people. This is one of the many ways there are for people to turn their personal stories into 'gospel.'

Prayer

Prayer is conversing with God – listening to and speaking with God. The listening comes first. Listening to God consists in accepting that God really communicates with us. The beauty of the world he created, the power of a parable told by Jesus, like 'the Good Samaritan', the goodness of someone we know, are all revelations of God and communications from God. People pray when they respond to these communications. It is the most natural thing in the world.

Speaking to God depends above all on paying careful attention to what he has communicated to us of himself. 'I bless you, Father, Lord of heaven and earth,'[14] is how Jesus starts one of his prayers, expressing his sense of who God is for him. Any of us can do the same, for example, by paying full attention to the power and sensitivity of God which we have just glimpsed in a glorious sunset. Prayer continues by responding further to the other things we notice about God as we continue to pay attention to him.

Conversations with God are not by any means always calm and delightful. They can involve a lot of anger and lamentation. The Book of Psalms, which is the prayer-book of God's people, contains prayers about the foe attacking the Holy City with axe and pickaxe,[15] as well as about the Lord as Good Shepherd. Prayer covers the whole range of human feeling. It is not just a means of growing in union with God. It is one of the principal ways of actually being in union with God.

Self-denial

An earlier chapter of this book has shown the need we have of disentanglement, and the topic is taken up again in the chapter on Twelve Steps Spirituality, 'Out of the Depths.' A readiness to deny oneself is essential for disentanglement from what does one harm. It is, if anything, more necessary for someone who is trying to grow spiritually in union with the crucified and risen Jesus. Some traditional spiritualities laid such emphasis on self-denial that they regarded it as almost the whole of the spiritual life. In the tradition of Christian gentleness, self-denial is appreciated, not only as an end in itself, but also as an indispensable means to spiritual growth.

Self-denial is a necessary means to spiritual growth because the personality cannot be opened up except by undertaking, for the sake of God, something that is great, difficult and painful. Nothing else can show what kind of a person one is, and what one's desires and fears really are. Fasting, hard and disciplined physical or other work, and obedience to a superior, are among the practices of self-denial, recalling St Paul's words quoted earlier about punishing his body and bringing it under control. These practices may have other goals too – saving money, perhaps. Their principal value, however, is to crack open the shell of the personality and to allow the person to enter into closer union with God, with others and with himself or herself.

Spiritual Direction

The practices of prayer and self-denial give rise to a practice sometimes called by the Irish name *anamcharadas* (soul-friendship) but more usually called spiritual direction. Neither prayer nor self-denial are easy to get right, because it is very difficult to attend to God in prayer, and even more difficult to preserve the balance of gentleness in self-denial. The task of the spiritual director is to help people to stay with what they are actually experiencing in prayer and with what they are actually aiming at in self-denial. The director helps the person to keep focused. He or she does not take over the person's life or any part of their life. The director does not 'direct' a person's life according to a plan, but listens with the person to hear where God is calling them. What the director has to do is sometimes extremely difficult – either overcoming his or her own temptation to intervene and sort things out, or challenging the directee's evasions. An even greater difficulty the director can have is staying on the spiritual level of the directee's relationship with God, rather than settling for easier and more natural issues. The existence of a ministry with that precise goal helps to keep the issue of spiritual growth before people's minds.

Retreats

The scriptural model for retreats is the withdrawal of Jesus and his disciples to a deserted place,[16] so that they could rest from their exhausting missionary work and spend time in prayer and reflection. To retreat means literally to withdraw or retire. In the history of the church, monasteries have been places of permanent withdrawal for the monks, where non-monks could join them for short periods. Since the sixteenth century, other religious houses besides monasteries began to offer residential retreats of, say, a week's or a month's duration. A particular form of retreat was offered by St Ignatius Loyola and the Jesuits, typically lasting thirty days, which aimed at enabling people to open themselves to God's grace for making an important decision or growing in the Christian life. A shorter, eight-day, retreat was promoted by other Catholic reformers in the tradition of St Francis de Sales. Somewhat later, renewal programmes known as 'missions' began to be organised in parishes, as a way of bringing retreats to people where they lived, and thereby reaching people who were poor. Retreats of all these kinds continue to be provided at the present time. Quite large numbers of people take part in them, in order to renew their Christian commitment. Similar practices are found in other Christian denominations besides the Catholic Church.

Retreats are occasions when long periods can be spent in prayer. In some retreats, a spiritual director can be met on a daily basis. His or her function is to help the retreatants to listen to what God is saying to them. Inevitably, it is well-off people with a good deal of spare time who are able to make residential retreats. However, directed retreats are now becoming available to people in their own parishes, so that many more people can avail of this important opportunity of grace.[17]

Sacramental Life

A core feature of the Christian religion is the sacramental system. The sacraments are religious rituals which bring people close to God, none more so than the two principal sacraments, baptism and eucharist. When a person is baptised, he or she becomes a child of God and a member of the body of Jesus Christ. When people take part in the celebration of the eucharist, they are effectively present with Mary and the beloved disciple and the repentant thief on Calvary, and with the disciples at the Last Supper. Two other sacraments complete baptism. They are confirmation, which gives the gift of the Holy Spirit, and the sacrament of reconciliation, which restores a repentant person to holiness lost by sin. The sacrament of the anointing of the sick gives people divine strength and sometimes physical healing when they are ill. Finally, what are known as the two social sacraments, ordination and marriage, provide the church with pastors, who are given the grace to care for God's people, and with married couples, who are given the grace to love each other and their children.

This 'sacramental system' provides very close union with Christ at key moments of life. Three of the sacraments place people in a unique relationship to Christ which lasts throughout life, and so they cannot be repeated. They are baptism, confirmation and ordination. All the sacraments, except baptism and reconciliation, require people receiving them to be in a state of grace or friendship with God. Whenever a sacrament is received in the right spirit, and is celebrated with due preparation, it produces a profound and memorable effect on the people involved. This has certainly been my experience, and it is why I count them among the most important means for growing spiritually.

Study

In the tradition of Christianity, not least in Ireland, hard intellectual work has always occupied an important place. Basically, this is the study of the 'sacred pages' or the scriptures. The 46 books of the Old Testament and the 27 of the New, are an extraordinarily rich and complex body of literature, which is recognised by the church as 'the word of God, inasmuch as it is consigned to writing under the inspiration of the divine Spirit.'[18] Many people of deep faith and enormous talent have spent and are spending their lives on all aspects of research into the sacred scriptures. This research has been not only very satisfying for them, but extremely helpful for everyone trying to grow in union with God.

Christians need not confine themselves to learning the conclusions of scholars, but can study the scriptures for themselves and get enlightenment and inspiration from them. There is a risk factor in this, because as the Second Letter of Peter warns concerning the writings of Paul, they contain some passages which 'uneducated and unbalanced people distort'.[19] But the church is there to correct any errors that may arise, so that the risk is small enough for everyone to be encouraged to read the bible for themselves.

Around the study of scripture, a vast range of other subjects has developed. Some of them are largely confined to specialists, others are, like the study of scripture, open to everyone. But, as in the case of any subject, an orderly and thorough foundation is necessary for these subjects, and dabbling in them may do little good or even much harm. The writing and reading explosion of recent decades has seen the publication of a number of books which anyone educationally well-grounded can see are completely wrong, but which can look exciting and even reasonable to people lacking the necessary background. So there is good reason to include methodical and thorough study of religion as a means to growing in union with God. Indeed, the study of any subject is beneficial to growth in union with God, the Creator of everything.

Moral Growth

It is a widespread opinion that Irish Christianity regards moral growth and spiritual growth as more or less the same thing. That would mean counting a person as growing spiritually as he or she was getting more patient, cleaner-living and more honest. The objection to that is obvious: you can be morally very good, but not very religious, let alone spiritual. So there is quite a swing away in modern spiritual direction from concentrating on people's moral issues to focusing on how people experience God. Spirituality has become less moralistic and more God-centred.

This is true, and it seems to be progress. But it does not mean that morality is not of great spiritual importance. The gospel and experience make it quite clear that moral issues really are central to spirituality. When the young man came to Jesus and asked what he needed to do to possess eternal life, Jesus replied by telling him to keep the commandments – 'you shall not kill, you shall not commit adultery, you shall not steal, you shall not give false witness, honour your father and your mother, and you shall love your neighbour as yourself.' And when the young man asked what else he should do, it was again in concrete behavioural terms that Jesus replied: 'Go sell what you possess and give the money to the poor.'[20] Experience confirms that the real beginning of people's spiritual living is often their conversion, that is, when they turn away from some sinful practice that has them enslaved.

The modern approach in spirituality is not by any means soft on morality. Rather, it is very strong on motivation, and starts there. While it is true that spirituality begins with conversion, conversion begins with motivation. And motivation begins with experience. It is often out of the experience of how awful they feel about it that people's motivation to overcome impurity grows. Or it may be a feeling of great inner attraction they experience when they hear the words of Jesus, 'Go away, and from this moment sin no more.'[21] Or one of many other experiences. The aim of modern spiritual direction is to enable people to listen to these experiences, and to allow their motivation to grow naturally out of them. Usually, there is little need to spell out the conclusions in detail, and when there is, it can as easily be to suggest moderation as to insist on action.

While I have been referring to this approach as 'modern', it is actually a classical Catholic approach, typical of the spirituality of Christian gentleness. In particular, the approach to prayer, to preaching and to practical spiritual living taught by St Vincent de Paul, placed all the emphasis on motivation. First dwell on the motives, the experienced motives, and then see exactly what to do. The emphasis is on motivation, on considerations whose whole point is that they lead to action. [22]

Avoiding Temptations

There is a reverse side to emphasising motivation in spiritual living, that is, also emphasising the avoidance of temptation. The permissiveness of today's society means that motives for sin are always being forced on people. For people to dwell on the attractiveness of moral conduct, they need some personal practices and social systems to prevent temptations getting too obtrusive. For many people, the initial move in spiritual living is a decision to avoid exposure to temptation. It is a kind of spiritual environmentalism, ridding one's surroundings of pollutants. There is a strange feeling around at the moment that people have to be tolerant of other people's efforts to corrupt them: for example, of the way pictures of affluence are used to advertise products, when, even in a comparatively wealthy country like Ireland, hundreds of thousands of people are forced to live in great poverty. The beginnings of a challenge to this odd kind of tolerance could be for people to eliminate from their own surroundings the propaganda for anti-spirituality. A personal or group policy along those lines can hardly be avoided by anyone seriously considering a spiritual life.

Church Life

The issue of avoiding temptation brings one up the question of social support. Spiritual living is not only deep in the individual person, but it also goes to the roots of society and culture. Spiritual living has a social dimension. There are many religious and other societies serving the social dimension of spirituality, but behind and around them all is the church. The church is a society founded by Jesus Christ himself, when he dispatched his apostles to preach his gospel to the poor of the world. It is permanent and world-wide. It owns the bible and the sacraments. It calls people to the highest holiness and the deepest humanity. One of the clearest proofs of the importance of the church for spiritual living is the ferocity with which the enemies of spirituality attack it.

Because the church is so necessary for spiritual living, people who want to live spiritually need to avail themselves of what the church has to offer. They also need to help the church to develop her potential for good, and to protect her from her enemies. Up to quite recently, church work of this kind was considered to be the preserve of full-time professional church people, mostly sisters, brothers and priests. While the dedication of clergy and religious is no less needed now than formerly, still the Acts of the Apostles show a church organised and spread by lay-people as well as by apostles and clergy. At the present time, the church is being largely served by lay people in Africa, South America and Asia. Comparative declericalisation of the church and offering lay-people the opportunity to use their gifts in the service of the church, are ways of fostering people's spiritual commitment.

Really spiritual commitment, however, shows not simply in the amount of energy put into organising church programmes. Spiritual commitment shows especially in the spirit in which church activities are carried on: a spirit of gentleness, kindness, peace, joy, humanity, love …, a spirit that respects and values poor people and a simple way of life. A spirit that rejects whatever is hard or haughty or hostile. This kind of spirit can be nourished only by sensitive motivation. It is a motivation that grows out of prayer and a very open and human bonding between people. A great deal would be lost if all the effort in restoring church life went into mighty projects, and not enough into the spirit with which the projects are carried through. History has a lesson in this respect. The courage and determination of the Spanish *conquistadores* of South America cannot be denied, nor can the fact that they had some elements of religious motivation. But they did enormous harm because of their lack of a really Christian spirit. Not even the amazing compassion of the waves of Spanish missionaries who succeeded them was enough to undo the harm the *conquistadores* did. The ordinary qualities of Christian kindness are as necessary for achieving great things for God and the human race as are courage, imagination and organising ability.

Social Involvement

My earliest personal involvement in what I consider to be spirituality was not in a strictly religious setting at all, but in the scout movement which aims at ordinary human values and simple fun. The greatest thing about that experience was that everything was so free and voluntary – you joined because you wanted to, you left if you wanted to. And nobody was making any money out of it. What there was in that movement, as I experienced it, was a real commitment to values, including religion, and to people, which was immensely attractive.

I see young people today benefiting not only from that movement, but also (like many of my contemporaries) from dozens and dozens of other movements and groups, from marching bands to hurling teams. And other people have always preferred to pursue their interests in less formal social groupings – getting together to build a boat or form a rock-group. I feel very deeply that passionate social commitments like these are necessary for spirituality. There has to be something wrong with a religion that is too exclusively religious. I don't know whether the Ephesians and the Colossians ever did anything like playing football matches against each other, but I would be rather relieved to learn that they did.

In saying all this, I am writing on the small page of one person's life what can also be written on the broad expanse of society as a whole. There is an immense range of human activities for people to commit themselves to, everything from street leagues to fashion competitions, and above that from administering the law to making the law. An eagerness to get involved in, or even to make a career out of, such social programmes is far from alien to spirituality. Social involvement is a proof of real spirituality, allowance being made for the temperamental difference between the activist and the observer. The Second Vatican Council's insist-ence on the value of human activity endorses social involvement more than any other kind of activity:

> Far from considering the conquests of man's genius and couraged as opposed to God's power as if he set himself up as a rival to the creator, Christians ought to be convinced that the achievements of the human race are a sign of God's greatness and the fulfilment of his mysterious design. With an increase in human power comes a broadening of responsibility on the part of individuals and communities; there is no question, then, of the Christian message inhibiting men from building up the world or making them disinterested in

the good of their fellows: on the contrary, it is an incentive to do these very things. [23]

Not alone does spiritual maturity impel people to the degree of social involvement that is appropriate to their gifts, but the social involvement enriches spirituality also. It allows spirituality to display its real worth. This can be seen from simple things like how much his Englishness enriched the Christianity of Thomas More, and how the African culture of the Uganda martyrs enriched their Christianity. But it can be seen most clearly, I think, in the life of Jesus himself. It is the way he lived in and belonged to his time and place that allow the humanity and divinity of Jesus to come across to us: the far-from-wealthy life-style of a journeyman roof-maker (or carpenter) and an itinerant religious teacher, the eye which was caught by a man sowing wheat in his field and a woman searching for her lost coin, the compassion of a man who met the funeral of a widow's only son at the town gate, and the courage of a person who was not afraid to confront the entire Jewish establishment and the Roman Empire. His involvement with the social order brought Jesus to Calvary, but it also made it possible for him to develop and make known every aspect of his character. He challenges his followers to that much commitment when he sends them out to 'make disciples of all nations.'

Notes

1. 1 Corinthians 9:24-27
2. Vatican 2, 'Constitution on the Church', n 11, in A Flannery (ed), *The Conciliar and Post-Conciliar Documents*, Dominican Publications, Dublin 1980, p 362.
3. cf. Titus 1:7: 'The president has to be irreproachable since he is God's representative.'
4. cf.Philippians 3:17: 'Brothers, be united in imitating me.'
5. Luke 3:10
6. John 4:29
7. Acts 2:37
8. James 1:23/24
9. Ephesians 6:4
10. See also what is said later, on self-denial.
11. Maurice Hayes, 'Social Problems and Social Attitudes: Northern Ireland', in *Good News in a Divided Society*, Dominican Publications, Dublin 1992, p 48. Hayes also reports that 'a recent survey of the family by an Australian anthropologist ... found increasing anxiety about the structure and nature of the family. Most people saw the family as the most important thing in their lives but

threatened by the struggle for economic survival, decline in living standards, rising crime rates and individualism.'

12. Exodus 33:11

13. *The Imitation of Christ*, trs Betty I.Knott, Fontana, Glasgow 1963, Book 3, ch 2. cf. also St Ignatius Loyola, *The Spiritual Exercises*, ed Puhl, n 15, as above.

14. Matthew 11:25

15. Psalm 73:5

16. Mark 6:31

17. The Autumn 1992 *Supplement to The Way* (London) deals entirely with retreats, and contains very useful material.

18. Vatican II, *Constitution on Revelation*, n 9.

19. 2 Peter 3:15

20. Matthew 19:16-22

21. John 8:11

22. This is known as 'the little method,' and one of the best accounts of it is given by Joseph M. Connors, SVD, in 'The Vincentian Homiletic Tradition', *The American Ecclesiastical Review*, 1958, vol 139.

23. Vatican II, The Church in the Modern World, n 34, as above.

24. Matthew 28:19

CHAPTER SEVEN

Out of the Depths

He snatched me from my powerful foe
From my enemies whose strength I could not match.
Psalm 17

'He descended into hell'
There is a disconcerting sentence in the Apostles Creed: *He de-scended into hell*. These words, as the new *Catechism of the Catholic Church* explains, describe how completely Christ has conquered death.[1] But when I hear them I am reminded of the fact that many people can say, knowing all too well what they mean, that they have been to hell, or been through hell. They are people recovering from addiction, especially but not exclusively substance addiction like alcoholism, and their recovering co-dependents.[2] I do not think it is wrong to give the words 'Jesus descended into hell' the additional meaning that God, when he became a human being, in some way shared their tragic experience. The degradation, anger and guilt which substance addiction brings to its victims and their co-dependents are absolutely real, and go as far as anything in human experience to suggesting what hell may be like.

The possibility of recovery from addiction is one of the great discoveries of the twentieth century. Over the last ten years or so, what are called 'Twelve Steps Spirituality' and 'Twelve Steps Retreats' have made their appearance. They are based on the twelve-step programme of recovery from addiction worked out by Alcoholics Anonymous. I want to include an account of Twelve Steps Spirituality in this book, because the hell it frees people from, and the joyful freedom it helps people to experience, give a very clear picture of spiritual living. I also have a shrewd idea that many of the spiritual problems facing world and church alike are problems of addiction.

Alcoholics Anonymous and the Twelve Steps
The spirit of Alcoholics Anonymous comes out most clearly in what may be called its 'basic operation': an addicted person standing before a group and saying 'My name is John (or Mary ...) and I am an alcoholic (or ...).' The idea of people doing that has entered the public imagination as typifying the late twentieth century. It has also entered literature, and many books, some of them

notable for their passion, their compassion and their solid research, have been published about Alcoholics Anonymous. One
of the most striking features of the movement is that, almost alone
of the major social movements originating in recent times, it directs peoples' attention to their need for spirituality and for God.

I made a visit to what is called 'middle America' in the late
1960s, in order to familiarise myself with the situation in which
many of the students I was teaching would be working. The person I was staying with introduced me to Alcoholics Anonymous,
because he considered that my familiarisation with America
would not be complete unless I had attended one of its meetings.
It is still a vivid memory for me: a group of twenty or thirty women
and men, many of whom looked physically quite ill, sat in an atmosphere of quiet determination. The face of the person who told
his story to the group that day could only be called ravaged,
which emphasised for me the importance and the difficulty of
what he was doing. He told how he had been a successful professional man who gradually drank his way out of his career and his
family life, and was nearing 'skid row' when someone showed
him how to start believing in himself again. He was a 'recovering'
alcoholic, and as I was later to learn would never consider himself
to be anything other than just 'recovering.' From that time on, I
could never look on 'recovery' as something easy, only as something much better than the alternative.

The Twelve Steps of the Alcoholics Anonymous programme,
which we will spend most of this chapter considering, originated
with 'Bill W.' and 'Dr Bob S.' in Akron, Ohio, in 1935. The Steps re-
flect the actual experience of their two authors, the experience of
recovering alcoholics. Over the past fifty years, the Twelve Steps
Programme has adopted a good deal of material from the experience of people in group and individual psychotherapy. The ver-
sion of the programme we will follow is found in the recovery
workbook entitled *12 Steps to Freedom*, edited by Kathleen W. [3]

Adaptations of the Twelve Steps for other Conditions
During the past few decades, the Twelve Steps Programme has
been adapted for other addictions besides alcoholism: for example, gambling, sexual addictions, addictions to work and power,
as well as co-dependency relating to these. Groups have started
specialising in these various conditions. There is even more social
resistance to regarding them as conditions in need of treatment
than in the case of alcoholism. Often, only bitter personal experience makes recovery programmes acceptable.

The 'basic operation' of all these programmes is the same: admitting before others, but in a safe group, that one has a personal condition that is out of control. Honesty, humility, faith and support are the common factors of Twelve Steps Programmes. Yet, as we shall see, Twelve Steps Programmes respect moral, religious and cultural diversity. They can be used by people who do not consider themselves spiritual at all.

Step One: Out of Control
The core experience of a person in any kind of addiction is that of being out of control. The person finds himself or herself locked in a behaviour pattern which they cannot get out of. Admitting that is the beginning of recovery. So, the First Step of the AA programme is, 'We admitted we were powerless over (alcoholism) (other people) (a compulsive pattern), and our lives had become unmanageable.'

Accepting that one has an unmanageable compulsion involves stopping the dodges people use in order to cope with addictions: denial, avoidance of the issue, intellectualisation, minimalisation, wise-cracking and so on. Recognising that one is dodging the issue can be difficult. People addicted to alcohol are often as committed to a false idea of themselves as honest, rational and normal people, as they are to the alcohol itself. As Gerald May says 'the mind's battle to deceive itself, with all its insidious tricks and strategies'[4] is part of the addicted person's experience. The addiction twists reality as much as is necessary to maintain itself.

Consequently, the first step is often taken when reality can be twisted no further: walking away from a fatal accident with the certainty of a criminal trial and the likelihood of prison, for example, or when the bank forecloses on a mortgage. The characteristic urgency of the Twelve Steps comes from having been at that extreme point of experience. That is why the Twelve Steps give rise to a *special* kind of spirituality. Otherwise, the awful experience on which the Twelve Steps are based would be for everyone, and somehow desirable as the basis of any spirituality. That kind of experience is not either a desirable or an inevitable part of life. Spirituality does not have to start where the Twelve Steps start. A sober realisation of what could happen is as good a base for spirituality as having to live through something terrible. It is better, in fact, because addictive and co-dependency experiences are very hard for people who have them to recognise. Very few addicted or co-dependent people get as far as the first step.

Recovery programmes have structures for making the first step easier: in particular, meetings at which one can hear other people making the First Step admission. Books and other means of social communication are also used, but the immediate, and yet anonymous, social encounter is the most effective method.

Step Two: Belief

The second step of the programme reads, '(We) came to believe that a Power greater than ourselves could restore us to sanity.' This is a very striking expression of faith. Still, Twelve Steps spirituality does not require its followers to believe in Jesus or in God, but only in a Power greater than themselves. The programme does not suggest who or what that Power is: that is up to the follower of the programme to discover for himself or herself. For many followers of the programme, belief in a power matching their own helplessness brings them to belief in God. They find from experience that he is the only one who can help them. As a result the Twelve Steps programme has a noticeably spiritual 'feel.'

Step Three: Decision

'(We) made a decision to turn our will and our life over to the care of God as we understand God.' This third step taken by the recovering addict is the move from knowing what to do, to actually doing it, like a swimmer taking the plunge. Recovering addicts are well aware how far belief is from action. This convinces them that they need to open up to spiritual power. As Kathleen W. puts it:

> Buried pain, rage, and fear we may discover within ourselves can be overwhelming, and reliance upon purely human forms of support may not be adequate, or sufficiently dependable to see us through. (People have an uncanny way of going on vacation or being preoccupied with their own issues when we depend on them instead of on our own internal resources.)[5]

Opening up to the spiritual power outside ourselves imeans recognising a place of spiritual receptivity inside ourselves. This is the rediscovery of the human soul. I do not think anyone today is highlighting the soul more clearly than proponents of the Twelve Steps.[6]

Using the *Serenity Prayer*, which is like a spiritual anthem for Alcoholics Anonymous, is one of the main ways of taking the third step:

> God grant me the serenity
> to accept those things

I cannot change,
Courage to change
those things I can,
and wisdom to know the difference!

Step Four: Fearless Moral Inventory
The first three steps launch the recovering person on to the most
demanding stage of the programme, steps four to six. Step four is,
'(We) made a searching and fearless moral inventory of ourselves.' In it, the recovering person tries to recognise exactly what
sort of a person he or she is: admitting dysfunctional behaviours
and attitudes, and, what is sometimes more difficult, admitting
what is unique and good about oneself. Praise is sometimes harder
to accept than blame. It is often harder for addicted or co-
dependent people to remember their good points, not because
they have not got any, but because people like that usually have a
strong streak of self-hatred which keeps their good points hidden.
An important part of recovery programmes is for people to discover how very much they like themselves, faults and all.

Step Five: Another Human Being
'We admitted to God, to ourselves, and to another human being
the exact nature of our wrongs.' To a large extent, the recovering
person is alone in taking the first four steps. At the fifth step he or
she shares with someone else what exactly is the matter with
them. The particular importance of this is to break the habit of
secretiveness that usually goes with addiction. Indeed, secretiveness characterises wrongdoing generally, which 'hates the light',
in the words of Jesus.[7] As well as breaking that habit, telling
someone else helps people to be more exact with themselves. A
vague description will make the other person uncomfortable, as if
they were being used as a means for further concealment. When
they demand a clearer picture, they help the recovering person.

Step Six: Letting God Remove Habits
'We became,' say the founders of AA about their experience, 'entirely willing to have God remove all these defects of character.'
Put like this, the sixth step seems quite shocking. It conflicts with
many people's idea of God as one who punishes. It also conflicts
with the often-heard slogan that 'alcoholism is a sickness'. Alcoholism is a sickness, but one that is cured by personal commitment as much as by treatment. What God does is help with the
commitment. He does as much as is needed. Asking for the help

one needs is the 'Sixth Step Prayer,' as the *Serenity Prayer* goes with the third step. Often the only intervening God has to do is breathe the inspiration, 'Go on! Continue your efforts.'

Step Seven: Humbly Asking

At the centre of the seventh step, '(We) humbly asked God to remove our shortcomings,' are humility and prayer. Humility has already been presented in Chapter Three as a central quality in spirituality. However, it is important for it to come up here again, because, in the context of addiction and co-dependency, there can be a kind of bogus humility. Real humility is, as Kathleen W. puts it, 'a genuinely positive quality.'[8] Among the dysfunctional tendencies that are sometimes mistaken for humility, are a tendency to put oneself down, and a tendency to minimise the progress there has already been in one's life. Our highly competitive society often lends support to the idea that people have achieved nothing unless they have achieved everything – that a footballer is no one, for instance, unless he has played for his county. In fact, he has already achieved much if he has enjoyed himself in the street leagues. Humility is being happy with the truth about oneself, and while it recognises one's failings, it does not 'awfulise' them. When a person is in the grip of false humility, it is often because of anger or shame picked up at an early stage of life when one has little control over oneself. Specialist help may be needed for that, and it is humility to admit such a need. It is also humility to spend time tending and reparenting one's 'inner child' – the child everyone always is.[9]

Prayer to one's Higher Power is the simplest and most natural expression of oneself: saying what one wants, asking for what one wants, and trying to admit the feelings that may be choking one up. I think that the Lord's Prayer itself is not so much a formula to recite, as Jesus modelling for us this kind of very simple praying. In it we ask to know our Father, to have our daily food, and not to be overwhelmed with guilt or anger or evil of any kind.

As well as expressing oneself in prayer, Kathleen W. suggests using some simple techniques of psychosynthesis. For example, visualising one of the defects one has, and then visualising oneself handing it over to God and letting go. She also suggests relaxation exercises, like having a bath or taking an unhurried walk. These help people to befriend themselves without feeding their addiction.

Step Eight: Persons we have harmed
Steps eight and nine widen somewhat the scope of recovery from addiction and co-dependency to consider people whom one may have harmed. Step eight reads: 'Make a list of all persons we have harmed and become willing to make amends to them all.' What this means is deciding to do our own part in healing relationships. It does not mean taking responsibility for other people and how they may behave, not even those we have harmed.

The first thing is to list those we are or have been related to, in different degrees of closeness. Perhaps the best way is to draw a series of concentric circles, divided into an upper and a lower half. The centre circle is oneself, the upper half of the remaining circles contains people one was related to in childhood, and the lower half contains people one is or has been related to in adult life. For example, the second circle contains mother and father in the upper half, spouse and children in the lower half.

Next, one tries to remember the ways in which one has harmed those in the various relationships. For example, did I attack them violently, by hitting or threatening them? Did I impose on them, by making them depend on me? Did I try to control or manipulate them? And finally, did I reject or participate in rejecting them?

As in step four, there is likely to be both resistance to admitting any guilt in relation to other people, and a tendency to confuse the issue by taking refuge in all-round self-effacing guilt: 'I'm just awful.' As a safeguard against these dodges, it is best to follow up a few things we definitely feel bad about and are fairly sure of. Other injuries we may have inflicted can be postponed for later consideration. But each time one works on the issue, there will be a harvest of resentment, shame and guilt to be noted and let go, as well as a crop of simple things that can be done in order to make amends – as simple perhaps as mentally wishing well to or praying for someone who has now gone out of one's life.

Often it is helpful to share issues of this kind with another person, perhaps the trusted confidant of step five. Simply doing that may be enough to clarify what can be done to make amends. Such a person will probably help us to realise that the one we most harmed in all these injustices was ourselves, and that making what amends we can means healing ourselves as much compensating anyone else.

Step Nine: Making Amends
The recovering person commits himself to taking appropriate action when he or she undertakes the ninth step: 'Make direct

amends to such people wherever possible, except when to do so would injure them or others.' Taking appropriate action is not revenge, for example on an person one is co-dependent with. Neither is it manipulation, like correcting an injustice without honestly meeting the injured party. The appropriate action is a genuine entry into a good relation with that person, and it depends a great deal on getting the timing and the approach right. Grace is needed for this. The recovering person has to ask his Higher Power for the grace of tact, as well as attending to his or her own feelings. The most important thing is not to make matters worse.

Step Ten: Continuing
The last three steps in the programme are called 'maintenance steps in recovery,' and are based on the fact that the addicted or codependent person is always in recovery. The process is never over as long as he or she lives. This is a point worth re-emphasising, as the''bargaining' mentality typical of addiction can lead a person to say to his Higher Power, 'I have done my bit, so if I am not recovered now it's your fault.'

What is more, the unceasing deviousness of addiction requires unceasing attention on the part of the person in recovery. It takes sharp wits to spot the new ways in which the addiction may be asserting itself. There is an ongoing process of trial and error, of which the basic ingredient is honest communication with oneself and with other people.

Taking new inventories from time to time is a way of keeping up the process. An inventory, though, is not supposed to be self-judging so much as 'just noticing.' It does not help to 'awfulise' either our mistakes or our deviousness.

Step Eleven: Prayer and Meditation
The eleventh step reads: 'Seek, through prayer and meditation, to improve our conscious contact with God as we understand God, praying only for knowledge of God's will for us and power to carry that out.' The practices of spirituality, whatever one's spirituality is, form an essential support for people in recovery. It enables them to remain in regular communication with their Higher Power, and with some of the deepest and most inspiring things in human culture and human nature. An authentic religion keeps the 'inner child' alert and responsive.

Those in recovery are especially sensitive to dysfunctional religious practices or people, that is, practices or people with too much in them that is insensitive, obsessive or wounded. Religion too needs to remain in recovery. It is not immune from being used as a disguise by addictions struggling to remain in existence.

Retreats, spiritual direction and even study courses may be more necessary for those in recovery than for other people, in order to preserve the fresh and childlike quality of their new-found spirituality. Imaginative meditation is good for preserving a fresh spirit. Still, even such exercises can become dehumanised. The important thing is for a recovering person to keep in steady contact with God and with his or her own spirit.

Step Twelve: Carrying the Message
The recovery programme involves reaching out to other people who are in need of it, and so the last of the Twelve Steps reads: 'Having had a spiritual awakening as a result of these steps, we try to carry this message to others and to practise these principles in all of our affairs.' This, as Kathleen W. says, 'is not based on a joyless sense of obligation.'[11] Still less is it based on projection or substituting outer concerns for doing one's own interior work. The twelfth step is constantly revitalised by the earlier steps. Like them, it aims mainly at freeing and enriching the recovering person. Being a 'Twelve Steps Missionary' is chiefly sharing one's own experience, and then being enriched by other people's experience.

The effects of the programme, freedom, warmth, communication and spirituality, deserve to be passed on to other people. They also call to be allowed penetrate into the various aspects of one's own life. It is important to mention this, because of the way addictions and co-dependent patterns try to maintain themselves in existence by 'migrating' from one aspect of life to another, and need to be pursued. Maintaining a steady openness and freedom in one's mind and heart is the best way to spread the good effects of the programme throughout one's life.

The Twelve Steps and Traditional Spirituality
Traditional spirituality has always battled against addiction, though not co-dependency, which was only discovered recently. The hardness of some spiritual traditions helps to break addictive habits. Even the gentleness of the tradition represented by this book is close to some aspects of the Twelve Steps. Examples are, the openness of Gregory's *Pastoral Rule* to the needs of people in every kind of situation, and to the prevailing conditions of society, and the readiness of the great contemplatives to reach up to God.

Particularly close to the Twelve Steps is the vision of St Vincent de Paul, that even in the most wretched human being there is the portrait of Jesus Christ. Vincent would not accept that the worst oppression, self-inflicted or otherwise, amounted to the final hell. The most crushed human spirit contained, he believed, the potential of the fullest human and even divine life. Twelve Steps spirituality can be grafted on to the traditional spirituality outlined in Chapter Three.

There is more to be said than that, however. The tradition of Christian gentleness actually needs the Twelve Steps. The humanity and delicacy that characterise Christian gentleness seem to suggest that all is well with the human situation, that it is not desperate. The Twelve Steps recognise that, quite the contrary, the human situation sometimes really is desperate. But they also hold that the resources are available for people to claw their way out of the abyss.

The discovery of co-dependence confirms this. The damage one person's addiction does to other people is such that a gentle kind of spirituality and religion cannot always repair it. That is not its function. A gentle spirituality cannot usually build upon personalities that are too deeply wounded. It needs them to be healed first, by something like the Twelve Steps. It is significant that, in the gospels, Jesus had a precursor, the fiery John, and that he was careful to align his ministry with John's.

Notes

1. *Catechisme de l'Eglise Catholique*, Mame - Librarie Editrice Vaticane, Paris 1992, nn 631-637.
2. Co-dependents are people who, as a result of not feeling safe in a relationship, adopt dysfunctional methods of coping. For example, they may deny their feelings, or not communicate, or take on a responsibility they are not able for. In the text, I frequently bracket co-dependents together with addicts, but I do not wish to suggest that all co-dependent people are addicts, or vice-versa. What is said in the text about addicted and co-dependent people often also applies to people who have been the victims of childhood physical or sexual abuse.
3. Published in 1991 by The Crossing Press, Freedom, California 95019. In keeping with their principle of anonymity, members of Alcoholics Anonymous do not give their full names.
4. *Addiction and Grace*, p 43.

5. *12 Steps to Freedom*, p 32.
6. The doctrine of the soul is also central to the theory and practice of psychosynthesis.
7. John 3:20
8. *12 Steps to Freedom*, p 81.
9. Among the many books available which deal with inner child work, may be mentioned John Bradshaw's *Homecoming*, Bantam, New York 1990.
10. *12 Steps to Freedom*, pp 82-3.
11. The same, p 138.

CHAPTER EIGHT

Spirituality and Dying

O precious in the eyes of the Lord
Is the death of his faithful.
Psalm 115

Tragedy at Christmas

It was Christmas Night. I was celebrating a midnight Mass for a packed church at an African village not far from the main road. Crowds of people back from the cities for the holiday filled the church. Endless lines of them danced up for the offertory. Choirs from different parts of the village out-sang each other with melodious African carols. Children slept contentedly in the altar-area. Altar servers in red and white replaced burning-out candles and moved around with books and incense. Celebration felt as if it would burst at any moment. Unexpectedly, another priest on his way to a village further on came up beside me and whispered, 'There are rumours of a bad accident on the road.' For me the rest of that Christmas Mass was filled with foreboding, as it went on for another hour of praying and dancing and singing.

I got to the road with some companions as soon as I could, to find the seminary's Toyota bus a crumpled wreck beside the parked unlighted tanker it had crashed into. The newly printed copies of the seminary magazine it had gone to the city to fetch littered the road. Another ten minutes brought us to the hospital morgue, where the bodies of the instantly-killed driver and his three companions were lying: two seminarians and the driver's brother. It is fifteen years since that Christmas night, but I find I can give my account of it now as clearly as I could then. A ghastly accident, as the papers said. One I was to tell about many times next day as I drove hundreds of miles to inform relatives and church authorities about what happened. An event full of sad details – a pair of new shoes in one of the bags, one of the victims writing in the magazine about the achievement of bringing it out, another dying within a mile of his own home. An event to wreck any Christmas celebration, and it did wreck many. And yet, the accident only echoed something I had heard in a talk many years before, that the stable at Bethlehem is in the shadow of Calvary: no room at the inn, the massacre of the children. I found that easier to believe, now. What is harder to realise is that Calvary is lit up by

118

Bethlehem. Even the ghastliest of accidents, made ghastlier by happening on Christmas Night, is transformed in its root by God's presence, and our reaching out towards that presence. There is, though, an amount of painful growing to struggle through from the root to the leaves, the flowers and the fruit, that prove how spirituality transforms both life and death.

If that accident had to happen, for me at least it was a grace that it happened at Christmas. Its timing forced me to recognise that Christmas is all about taming the monsters of death and inhumanity. And it also led me to accept that real spiritual growth means reaching a point where disaster and celebration can exist together in the same person, with peace as the result, not madness. As I drove around Eastern Nigeria that Christmas Day, I was taught a lesson – more than I realised at the time – about how to accept calamity. People accepted it in an attitude conditioned by a civil war that was still fresh in their memories, but stemming mainly from thousands of years of the struggle between life and death in the villages of the rain forest, and given its purest refinement in the gospel accepted a generation or so before.

Faith and Eternal Life

It is part of the Christian faith that union with God cannot be complete until a person has died. In other words, full spirituality is only possible when one is dead. At times, this doctrine, and the certainty that it is true, are terrifying. At other times, for example when one has been bereaved, it is a consoling doctrine. Beyond the comfort and the dread there is something else. The fact that spiritual fulfilment comes only when a person has died, turns our natural view of things upside down. It is a crushing blow to our confident human self-sufficiency. Or, to put the matter another way, the fact that death must precede spiritual fulfilment means that humans are not self-sufficient. That is a difficult thing for many people to accept today.

I think that I would be among those who shrug off this central teaching of Christianity, if I had not had my attention drawn to a significant theoretical point: the difference between what is necessary and what is sufficient. It is one thing to say that a full life between birth and death is not sufficient for personal fulfilment. That is indeed the case. But it is not the same to say, and it is not true to say, that a full human life is not necessary for personal fulfilment, that is, spiritual fulfilment. It is necessary. Complete humanness is essential for complete spirituality. Living as fully human a life as I can is not something I can forego in view of eter-

nal happiness after death. Just the opposite. My spiritual fulfilment depends entirely on my making a success of human living.
Christianity is (if I may use the word) a formula, *the* formula, for
making a success of human life. Its formula can be reduced to a
single word, love: love of others, love of self, love of God. That is
what spirituality is all about. And the reason why spirituality is
fulfilled after death is that death is the moment when we become
capable of entering fully into loving union with God. Which we
shall do, if only we have used this life to become spiritual enough,
that is, loving enough.

I am grateful to those who taught me my academic courses for
helping me to see how human life and eternal life are related. But
I am well aware from my own and other people's experience that
seeing that point is only the start. In fact, it is not where people
who are less intellectually inclined than I am will want to start.
The reality of human living, and the starting-point for (I suspect)
most people as they try to line up human life and eternal life, is
the give and take of human relationships, including the human-
divine relationship. I listened recently to a speaker on BBC radio
describe the life and death of a County Tyrone woman whose five
sons had emigrated from Ireland long before. Her life was the joy
and pain of bringing them up after their father's early death, the
sorrow of seeing them leave home, so hopefully one after another,
her own hope as Christmas approached of a card from them, the
sadness when some did not remember, the delight at those who
did, the deep loneliness, and the unutterable forgiving love. In
that radio programme, the woman and her sons had a voice to
speak for them, and that voice had listeners because it spoke of
the innermost reality of human life, the laughter and the groaning
of people's hearts in their relationships with one another. The
great task facing the human race, I feel, is to get us to live at the
level of the heart. If it only takes a little thought, a radio programme, well and good. If not even that is needed, so much the
better. But for nearly everyone, something is needed to move us
in the direction of the heart. Which is why God has entered his
world and established his church.

The life of personal relationships is never ended, least of all by
death which so often snatches people away unexpectedly. And
the relationship with God has hardly begun when we come to die,
however much progress we have made in it. All our other relationships reach a new depth as the relationship with God deepens
into eternal life. Eternity hardly seems long enough for the mystery of living together with God to unfold itself.

Faith and Damnation: a seventh person

There is an awesome reality, which does not bear thinking about, but which cannot be ignored, and that is the possibility of eternal damnation. It is the reverse side of the gospel, or rather, the gospel is the good news that damnation can easily be avoided.

What does being damned mean? It means, first, a person not ceasing to exist when he dies, any more than a person who is saved does. And it also means a person not entering into the loving companionship of God and of those who have allowed love to rule their lives. Instead, damned people have to endure their own company, just as an addicted person does. Being damned does not, I think, necessarily mean any positive punishment, or any fire other than unending frustration and shame. Damnation is not inflicted by God, it is self-inflicted. Moreover, there is nowhere any proof that any particular human being has been or will be damned, only that anyone will be who has not opened himself or herself to the gospel of love.

It has to be admitted, at least by me from my experience of being myself, that the possibility of closing oneself off to the gospel of love is a real one. It can happen in any number of ways – the kinds of anti-spirituality described earlier no doubt are some of the ways. But, to give some experiential weight to the possibility of damnation, consider the following sketch account of an imaginary person, like the six people in Chapter One.

Godwin

Godwin is rich. At least, he is rich now, though he has twice been declared bankrupt. A lucky break with a heroin shipment started him off again after the second time, though he has to be careful to do his spending out of sight of police and tax inspectors. He was born in a well-to-do family, and could have whatever he wanted as a boy. Physically he is very strong, and he has a quick mind. In his first year at university, he and the set he belonged to decided that God and religion counted for precisely nothing. That did not stop him having a society wedding in a fashionable church, but it does help explain why he snapped up the chance of a divorce when his neglected and alcoholic wife sought comfort in someone else's arms five years later. Since then he has been free to live as a citizen of the world. Just at this moment he is becoming angry at being made to wait fifteen minutes beyond the time of his appointment with a specialist. He wants to have his persistent cough investigated – Godwin has no wish to go to an early grave.

What can the loving God do about Godwin? That seems an absurd question, because God is supposed to be able to do everything. But the real absurdity is in the idea that God could save anyone who did not want to be saved. If my Godwin turns out to be a person who never existed, or never persisted in his self-absorbtion, then he is not damned. But otherwise he surely is, in the sense of having to live with himself for ever.

Some religions hold that there is a second chance for people like Godwin, or a series of 'reincarnations.' What is wrong with that idea is that it undermines the value of the human birth-to-death life that is the only one we know. This is the only life there is for people to make of themselves whatever they are going to be. It is the life that God made his own in Jesus Christ. It is not a life in which being saved is particularly difficult. Being childlike, as Jesus repeatedly says, is the key to being saved. A real openness to God, even if a person has not got a very clear idea of God but does respect the human beings whom God made in the divine image, is all that the loving God looks for in a person.[1] Being saved is natural, being damned is perverse. But the Godwin story, and people's own experience of what they can do and neglect to do, show that the perversion is a real possibility.

Purgatory
In the world where I grew up, purgatory was one of the things we were most conscious of. One of the religious duties that was taken most seriously was the 'gaining of indulgences' for people who had died and who were 'in purgatory'. Repeated visits were made to churches in November to gain these indulgences, and the month of November was (and still is) considered a special time of fasting by many people. When I went to Africa, I found the same sense of obligation to family members who had died, and the same practice of praying for them to be released from their purgatory.

All of this is very little spoken of nowadays, and it seems almost incredible to young people. The idea of purgatory, by which I mean the sense that people who die might not be immediately ready for heaven, is often forgotten in funeral Masses, with white vestments being worn, and the good qualities of the deceased person being so much spoken of even in the homily of the Mass that it is almost as if the person was being canonised.

I think there is a valid point in this deep shift of people's feelings and even their beliefs about what happens after death. The point mentioned earlier in connection with 'reincarnation' applies also to an exaggerated view of purgatory. When too much is made of purgatory as a place of sanctification before a person is ready for heaven, the importance of this life as the place where we 'work out our salvation with fear and trembling'[2] is diminished. And yet I think that we are in danger of making a mistake by ignoring purgatory, as the Protestant reformers did.

Purgatory is actually a name for a process, not a place. The process of purgatory (or purgation, or cleansing, or sanctification) is the central process of the whole Christian life. It goes on with steadily increasing intensity in the life of anyone who is serious about their religion. It is described in detail by St John of the Cross: an active and a passive process, first at the level of sense and then at the level of the spirit, in which the individual person cooperates lovingly with God who transforms the person.[3]

What is called 'purgatory' in the sense of purgatory-after-death is quite simply the fact that those who have begun the process of purification during their lives have not necessarily completed it before they die. Sanctification must be complete before a person can be fully united with God and the saints. Hence purgatory after death. It is painful in much the same way as purification in this life is – John of the Cross calls that 'terrible.' The prayer of other people for the continued spiritual growth of those who have died is a very good thing, as is prayer for the spiritual growth of those still alive.

My fear is that the eclipsing of purgatory in the popular mind may signify an underestimate of what it costs to be a Christian. Being a Christian is not impossibly difficult, but it needs much more than a casual approach. I have the feeling that there is something casual about the playing down of purgatory. Those who have died, with some exceptions, need prayer, and even indulgences, as much as those who haven't.

Quite a number of people have told me how close they feel to parents, sisters, brothers, spouses or children who have died. Apart from this being a natural part of bereavement, it also seems to me a genuine faith-reality. Even if people who have died are undergoing purgatory, they are closer to themselves, to us and to God than we who are alive are: and they keep on getting closer as they progress towards full union with God. A person who is united to God is as close to us as God is. It seems completely natural then for someone to pray to, and not just for, their loved ones who have died. While it is true that people have dark secrets, unknown even to their closest friends, there is no reason to expect anyone to be damned unless they show signs of being somewhat like the Godwin I described above. So our dead friends can be prayed to. My impression is that there is not much need to encourage people to pray to their loved ones who have died, as they often do so quite spontaneously. What may be necessary is to discourage religious purists from trying to stop them. The point can be made like this. People who honestly want to go to heaven certainly will. Then, like Thérèse of Lisieux, they 'will spend their heaven doing good on earth.' Which being the case, it must be right to pray to them.

Care for the Dying
People's deaths cause very different reactions in other people. The differences are close to shocking. The death of an enemy in a war situation or something like it, can cause satisfaction even to very mild people. The death of a patient is difficult for some members of the medical professions to cope with. The death of a spouse or close relative can be shattering, one of the best-known historical instances being the effect on the English Queen Victoria of the death of her husband Albert. But the hospice movement which is gathering new strength today, and the care of Mother Teresa and her companions for homeless people dying in the streets of Calcutta, show a completely different and much more human response to death. And many bereaved people have learned for themselves, or been helped by others to learn, the wonder of staying with their loved ones and tending them as they die. These are not, of course, entirely new developments. They are as old as Christianity and indeed as humanity itself. Christianity especially recognises the dignity of the time when a person is moving towards eternal life, but even to ordinary human feeling there is something almost baby-like in the appeal of a dying person.

 I am conscious of how hard it is to reconcile these opposing reactions to death, which are sometimes experienced by the same people. As I have described them, one attitude looks negative and wrong, the other positive and very much right. And yet the attitude of a person towards the death of an enemy, or the attitude of a medical person towards the death of a patient, or the attitude of a Victoria, is not just a negative attitude. It is an extreme form of an attitude that is basically right. Enmity is based on what is perceived as injustice. Being crushed by the loss of a patient, or still more a relative, is based on a positive attitude towards the person. So even the 'negative' attitude cannot be completely rejected. I feel that bringing together these two conflicting attitudes is the kind of issue that needs to be dealt with in spiritual reflections, for instance, in sermons at the funerals of the victims of terrorism, or in on-to-one conversations with people who experience such conflict within themselves. The task of drawing such opposing attitudes together is difficult, but suppressing either of them is only driving the conflict into the unconscious mind. People need tactful help to face the issue. By 'tact' I mean a listening attitude to make sure that the person trying to help really knows what the other person (or community) thinks and feels.

What is needed in the person who is trying to help someone coming near death is a similar undemanding presence, aimed not at solving the dying person's problems for them, but at just being there for them when, and only when, one is wanted by them. The dying person doesn't want to be abandoned, but neither do they want to be, as it were, haunted. The issue of their own death which they are facing can help them to realise what is going on much better than those tending them. Simple kindness and intelligent attention to the person who is dying will usually help the watcher or attendant to know what to do and say. The following incident shows what I have in mind.

A priest I knew was dying at a relatively early age. Much of his life had been taken up in administration, and he was well known to be very secretive about his feelings, though apparently the person looking after him did not know that. At one point, the attendant heard him saying quite distinctly,'I'm finished, I'm finished, I'm finished.' The attendant said, 'What are you finished, Father?', and he immediately replied, 'I'm finished the accounts.'

That conversation was, I think, the last chance the man had to come to terms in a fully human way with his own dying, and my reading of the incident, as I was told it, is that the chance was completely missed. The dying man was quite clearly expressing his sense that his life was over. But the person attending him missed that, and interpreted his words in an almost jocular response, 'What have you finished?' or 'What job have you finished?' As quick as a flash, the dying man joined in the game, mentioned a job (surely far from his mind at that moment) and the opportunity was gone for ever. Had the person looking after him simply sat down beside him and attentively reflected back to him, 'You feel that you have finished, Father', who knows what a weight of regret, or more likely, knowing the man, of gratitude for a life well spent, the dying person might have been able to express. It would have been, as it were, his dying song. The attendant may not be altogether blamed: it might have taken almost superhuman tact to avoid triggering some defensiveness in the dying man. But

I think the incident does show the kind of sensitive love that is needed in people who attend the dying.

Preparing for Death
The last thing people want to hear about when they become dangerously ill, very often, is preparing for death. That is only natural, because the body's curative processes are struggling against illness, and the mind is correspondingly rejecting the idea of death. At the same time, the body and the mind together usually do have a sense of when death is approaching, as with the person I just described. Because of this, people prepare for death almost by a spontaneous process, even if they are often glad to invite the assistance of someone else. The spontaneous process will probably not be smooth, as Elizabeth Kubler-Ross has shown in her book, *On Death and Dying*.[4] But it does tend to happen naturally, and to end in resignation and peace.

What I have in mind in this section is longer-term preparation for death. Long-term preparation is really an aspect of life as a whole. It is something for young people as well as for very old people. Behind this life-long preparation for death is the awareness that , such being the force of habit, as we live, so we shall die, and that habits grow stronger, not weaker, the longer we live. The rule, 'live today as if you were to die tomorrow' is a wise one, even though it can be put to the service of unspirituality or antispirituality, as in 'eat, drink and be merry, for tomorrow we die'. A clear-eyed vision of what human life is about can make the fact of approaching death a reason for living at each moment as kindly and as honestly as possible. Some contemporary secular thinkers have defined human existence as 'being-unto-death'[5] in order to make that point. Having that kind of attitude to life is, I believe, what preparing for death essentially means.

At a lower level of urgency, preparing for death means looking at various pieces of 'unfinished business' in one's life. Naturally, it is as well to get these finished at a reasonably early stage. Otherwise, as life goes on, there may be just too many pieces of unfinished business and too little energy or time to finish them. Such unfinished business could be ruptured relationships that might need reconciliation or closure, unresolved issues in one's own personal life, such as guilt or resentment, and professional or cultural projects, whether aimed at personal development or the good of society. When people manage to attend to things like this in time to complete them satisfactorily, they can face their end with fewer regrets. And they will provide those around them with examples of living life to the full.

Preparing for death has a spiritual side, or a mystical side. The biggest thing in anyone's life is their relationship with God, which is uniquely personal to everyone. It is intended by God to reach a certain maturity in this life, and so it needs attention at every stage of life. But the spiritual side of life has its specially sensitive moments, like first communion or marriage or mid-life, starting a new venture or retirement. At moments like these it becomes more intense. They are opportunities for more direct personal intimacy with Jesus as one's saviour. And there is, as we have seen in earlier chapters of this book, progress through different stages of a person's union with Jesus: he is the one who releases one from entrapment, the one who inspires and supports one in personal growth, the one who invites us to share his suffering for the sake of the world, and the one who raises people up to a new life of freedom when they share his Calvary experience. Staying with the process of mystical union with Christ in all its stages is the principal way God has given the human race to prepare for death. This mystical union is far from being a life of sheer bliss. It goes through the desert and it carries the cross. As Thomas Keating puts it, 'we plug into the divine energy by consent, not by feeling or experience. This energy is totally available all the time on one condition – the consent of faith.'[6] But the spiritual life also knows its moments of intense joy, far greater than anything else available in the world. It is when the spiritual life comes to its fulfilment in heaven that people will know what it is to be completely human.

Heaven, God and Spirituality

Heaven is the place or condition in which everyone will spend almost their entire existence, unless they set their minds against it. And yet everyone's desires, ambitions, fears and skills are tied up with the stage of life ending with death. The world is the womb in which a person is painstakingly and painfully put together so as to be born into heaven, but all we can think in terms of is this world.

Even though it is only in terms of this-worldly experience that we can think, it is sometimes necessary to think about heaven. For one thing, we need to convince ourselves that it really exists and that it is desirable. This is especially necessary when someone is faced with the prospect of someone close to them dying, or dying himself. For another thing, the whole value of religion and the whole possibility of life being ultimately good depends on the final outcome being heavenly. Otherwise, what is the good of anything?

As I read the scriptures, they contain two kinds of account of what heaven is like. There are imaginative accounts and there are statements (usually very brief) which seem to catch something of the essence of heavenly existence. The principal example of the latter is: 'His servants ... will see him [God] face to face.'[7] Or, as a prayer in Mass for the Dead expresses it, 'On that day we shall see you, our God, as you are. We shall become like you ...'[8] Writers often use the words 'beatific vision', that is, 'sight which makes us completely happy', to describe heaven. The best known examples of *imaginative* descriptions of heaven are in the Book of Revelation, which describes heaven as a solemn liturgical celebration, and sometimes as a city in which all needs are satisfied by God himself and there is nothing but pure joy.[9]

I am inclined to think that the scriptural writers must have imagined heaven more in terms of what they missed on earth than in terms of what they actually experienced. The Mediterranean port cities, where Christianity took root in the first century, were as ruthless and squalid as any city today, with the small Christian churches providing oases of peace, though even they were subject to tension and pressure. The Christians dreamed of a liturgy as splendid as that of the recently destroyed Temple of Jerusalem, but they did not have, and would not have for hundreds of years, any churches of their own. They dreamed of a peaceful place to live, where God's will would be done 'as it is in heaven'. In the meantime, they made what contribution they could to creating a reflection of heaven on earth, by letting people see the beauty of Christian morality and by supporting the just laws and legitimate rulers of the places where they lived. They developed a liturgy and an inner church life to provide them with inspiration and refreshment in the face of oppression. They sought to create a life among themselves that would embody as many as possible of the qualities of God's kingdom, a kingdom of 'justice, love and peace.' The imaginative Christian vision of heaven fired, and still fires, the social involvement of Christians.

The other kind of statement about heaven, the effort to express the very essence of heavenly life, has, I believe, an even deeper impact on Christian life. Seeing God face to face, because we are like him, is the core of spirituality. Almost everyone knows what it is to catch a glimpse of one they love. Even people who cannot see know what joy it is to have a kind and interesting person in their company, if only for a moment. God is the personal being we most love, although, as this book has described, awakening that love takes a long struggle. God is the personal being who most loves us and who is most excitingly interesting. God's personal attractiveness is so great that it can absorb and delight the human race eternally. We have to live not by vision, but by faith, in the present life. The purpose of this is to allow our power of love and our longing for God to grow, and to prepare us for the everlastingly exciting life of heaven.

Notes

1. Matthew 25: 31-46
2. Philippians 2:12
3. See, *The Dark Night*, Books I and II, in Kavanaugh & Rodriguez, trs, *The Collected Works of St John of the Cross*, Institute of Carmelite Studies, Washington 1979.
4. E. Kubler-Ross, *On Death and Dying*, Macmillan, New York, 1969.
5. For example, the philosopher Martin Heidegger. cf. his *Being and Time*, trs Macquarrie & Robinson, Oxford 1973, pp 279ff.
6. *Awakenings*, HarperCollins, New York, 1991, p 48.
7. Revelation 22:4
8. Eucharistic Prayer III.
9. See Revelation, chapters 4 & 5, and 21 & 22.

Epilogue

This book began writing itself inside me several years ago when I was on my way back to Ireland from Africa, where I had spent quite a long time as a missionary. On the bus-journey across Nigeria, I was reading Peter Brown's biography of St Augustine.* The desire to get hold of my life as it had been up to then, somewhat as Augustine did in his *Confessions*, began to attract me. In Genoa, which is a sacred place for anyone in my spiritual tradition, because almost an entire community of Vincentians was wiped out there in St Vincent's time as they ministered to plague victims, I bought a pad and started writing. That venture came to nothing. Over the next few years, as I learned more about myself, and had the privilege of ministering to men and women of all ages and conditions in the intimate priestly ministry of spiritual direction, I gradually acquired the confidence I needed to write this book, and I was glad of the opportunity when it arose.

All I have tried to say in *You Are Mine* is that Catholic Christianity is the way to live, and that no one need have any fear of either travelling to the ends of the earth or staying at home to tell people that, from his own experience. Whoever does that will hear from strangers how much they already know of the gospel, from their experience. Doing that will not make him Personality of the Year if that is not something he is in line for anyway. What it will do is to make him into somebody in whom God, his angels and other people will take great delight. It is a kind of life for anyone to enjoy immensely.

* Brown, Peter, *Augustine of Hippo*, Faber & Faber, London 1975 (1967).

Selected Bibliography

Assagioli, Roberto, *Psychosynthesis*, The Aquarian Press, Welling-borough, Northamptonshire 1990 (1965)
> This is a popular handbook in psychotherapy, one of whose main values is the inclusion of many techniques for people to use in overcoming their personal deficiencies, as well as an account of the theoretical basis of psychotherapy. Much of what the book contains is reminiscent of traditional asceticism.

Barry, William, *God and You*, Paulist Press, New York 1987
> This book is a clear and helpful introduction to contemporary Ignatian spirituality.

Bredin, Eamon, *Disturbing the Peace*, Columba Press, Dublin 1985
> In this work of biblical theology, the author establishes the capacity of faith in Jesus Christ to transform the world.

Bro, Bernard, *The Little Way*, DLT, London 1982 (1979)
> This short book on the spirituality of Thérèse of Lisieux did much to rescue her from the 'little rose girl' image. 'The only way of appreciating Therese of Lisieux today is by adding her to the company of Marx, Nietzsche, and Freud. It is the same battle all along the line: man confronting the abyss ' (p 13).

Brown, Peter, *Augustine of Hippo*, Faber & Faber, London 1975
> This is a classic biography of one of the great formative figures of the Christian West. It illustrates the close bond between Christianity and deep culture, and yet the powerlessness of even cultivated Christianity in the face of the invading hordes of Vandals.

Brunot, Amadee, *St Paul and his Message*, Burns & Oates, London, 1959
> Paul is stormy, difficult, warmhearted and full of ideas. He has made a deeper mark on the history of Christianity than almost anyone else. Those who are trying to live Christianity need to have a sympathetic understanding of him. This is only one of many good biographies.

Carne, Patrick, *Don't Call It Love*, Bantam Books, New York 1991
This book describes how the Twelve Steps (cf. Ch 7 above) can be used as an approach to what used to be called depravity, but is now recognised as often being an addiction in the area of sexuality.

Casey, Michael, *What are we at?*, Columba Press, Dublin 1992
This book, by a Dublin curate, is alive with the thrill of meeting God in vulnerable people and helping them to find their own salvation. 'The spirit and reality of the gospel incubates in the bones and marrow of Dublin working-class people' (p 43).

Corish, Patrick, *The Irish Catholic Experience*, Gill & Macmillan, Dublin 1986 (1985)
Monsignor Corish's book does more than, perhaps, any other to capture the religious experience of the Irish people as a whole, Gaelic and anglicised, rural and urban, ancient, medieval and modern. It does so with a sensitive appreciation of the individual people involved in the story. Every nation's spiritual journey could do with being written up like this.

Dalrymple, John, *Simple Prayer*, DLT, London 1984
This is as good an expression as one may come across of the way the stages of growth in union with God unfold in the life of a busy and likeable pastoral priest.

De Mello, Anthony, *Sadhana*, Image Books, New York 1984
The majority of the human race have, for thousands of years, lived in Asia, and have been largely untouched by Christianity. De Mello in this book makes the benefits of Asiatic culture's attempts to reach God available to westerners. He helps people to rediscover the place of the body in prayer.

Doherty, James, *It's Never the Same*, Veritas, Dublin 1988
The shadow of the cross is there for anyone trying to live for God. This book is about Fr Jimmy Doherty's multiple sclerosis. But it also gives some idea of how what restricts the body can set the spirit free.

Doherty, James, *They Made Me a Priest*, Columba Press, Dublin 1992
Written to counteract some negative publicity the priesthood has lately been receiving, this book is based on the author's experiences. For all that, it is not stuck in the past. 'We are not priests alone, we hold priesthood with Jesus Christ and with the brotherhood of priests and with the priesthood of the laity, and, lest we forget, the women are as much part of the priesthood of the laity as the men' (p 105/6).

Faber, Heije, *Psychology of Religion*, Westminster Press, Philadelphia, USA, 1975

The negative effect of psychology, especially Freudian psychology, has been much insisted on, and this powerfully reasoned and very well-informed book by a Dutch psychologist does something to restore the balance. It is not purely academic, but suggests ways forward in the present situation. 'The representatives of both patterns [the traditional church and the younger people] give the impression of being bound always to react negatively towards one another. Each experiences the other as a threat. I think it is essential for the representatives of the two patterns to arrive at positive communication with one another' (p 323/4).

Francis de Sales, *An Introduction to the Devout Life*, (ed P. Toon,) Hodder & Stoughton, London 1988

Although this book was written nearly four centuries ago, for anyone able to make some historical adjustments it can still lead to a deep understanding of what is involved in living for God in an everyday setting.

Grosch, Gerald, *Quest for Sanctity*, Michael Glazier, Wilmington, Delaware, USA, 1988

This book traces the stages of spiritual growth in highly experiential terms, based on the author's years in the ministry of spiritual direction.

Hughes, Gerard, *God of Surprises*, DLT, London, 1988 (1985)

Hughes writes with a keen sense of the challenge of Christian living today, and this book is an inviting and practical introduction to spirituality.

Ignatius of Loyola, *The Spiritual Exercises*, ed L. Puhl SJ, Loyola University Press, Chicago 1951

The frequently made point that this is not so much a work to be read as referred to is valid enough. But careful reading of the Exercises can be illuminating, for example when one discovers that the aim of the Exercises is to help people to make decisions as freely as possible (n 21).

Jamart, Francois, *Complete Spiritual Doctrine of St Thérèse of Lisieux*, Alba House, New York 1961

Jamart's somewhat technical synthesis of the writings of Thérèse of Lisieux is a useful resource for anyone wanting to study her.

John of the Cross, *The Complete Works of St John of the Cross*, trs Kavanaugh & Rodriguez, Institute of Carmelite Studies, Washington DC 1979
> This is a very readable translation of John's poetry and prose, and is valuable for anyone who wants to read themselves gradually into this most attractive and perceptive spiritual master.

Keating, Thomas, *Awakenings*, Harper & Row, New York 1991
> This is a book of vignettes of human experience, from a biblical perspective, and it represents what is best in the application of modern biblical theology. It consists of personal reflections on the mysteries and sayings of Christ.

Kubler-Ross, Elizabeth, *On Death and Dying*, Macmillan, New York, 1969
> This celebrated book is a classic of pastoral and medical care, and testifies to the enormous contribution of women to the discovery of what it is to be human.

Laplace, Jean, *Preparing for Spiritual Direction*, Franciscan Herald Press, Chicago, 1975 (1967)
> As the title of this book indicates, it is intended to give perspectives for spiritual directors. Its central focus is on the freedom of the person being directed, and the director's role in fostering such freedom.

Leclercq, J., Vandenbrouke, F., Bouyer, L., *The Spirituality of the Middle Ages*, Burns & Oates, London 1968
> This is a very scholarly and quite technical book, but it has no equal in English for anyone who wants to grasp the overall movement of Christian spirituality in the middle thousand years of its history.

Martini, Carlo, *After Some Years*, Veritas, Dublin 1991
> This is another application of the learning of an outstanding scripture scholar to the every day task of living a Christian life in the contemporary world. The author is very conscious of the modern Christian's need for an inner source of strength: 'Without a profound awareness of call, the personality cannot survive the uncertainties of a merely pragmatic definition of self' (p 69).

May, Gerald, *Addiction and Grace*, Harper & Row, San Francisco 1988
> May's background in psychiatry and his appreciation of the saving power of religion, combined with his gift for writing

very well, have made this book something of a classic of contemporary spirituality.

May, Gerald, *The Awakened Heart*, Harper & Row, San Francisco
1991
In this sequel to the last title, May switches his focus to love as
the central reality in human life and in religion, and provides
what must be among the most appealing expressions of Christianity at the present time.

McNamara, Vincent, *Faith and Ethics*, Gill & Macmillan, Dublin
1985
This book explores the basis of moral living, and shows that the
issues are not altogether simple. It is especially powerful on the
importance of motivation in action, and in its suggestion that
love (agape) , far from being exclusively Christian, sums up the
deep humanness of Christianity.

Neary, Michael, *Our Hide and Seek God* , Mercier Press, Cork 1990
This book is an attractive example of scriptural learning at the
service of men and women, and in this case especially priests,
who are trying to live for God.

Nicholl, Donald, *Holiness*, DLT, London 1987 (1982)
This is a refreshingly-written book based equally on learning
and on interesting personal experience. Its approach is not exclusively Christian.

Nouwen, Henri, *Reaching Out*, Collins, Glasgow 1976
Henri Nouwen, a psychologict and a priest, has a special gift
for interpreting the essence of spiritual and pastoral movements, and showing the essential unity of the spiritual quest.
This is one of several books he has written on contemporary
monasticism.

Nouwen, Henri, *Creative Ministry*, Image Books, New York 1978
In this book, Nouwen deals especially with ministry to sick
people and the self-discovery of the minister.

Patrick, St., *The Letters of St Patrick*, ed Conneely, Daniel, and Bast-
able, Patrick, An Sagart, Maynooth 1993
'I, Patrick, a sinner, unlettered' are the opening words of the
personal testament of a great integrator. Patrick know how to
unite Roman and non-Roman worlds, and how to win over his
own persecutors. His deep consciousness of the presence of
God in scripture and in experience compelled him to make
'monks and virgins of Christ' of the sons and daughters of Irish

chieftains (Confession of Grace, n 41) and to state of himself, 'I live for my God to teach the heathens' (Letter Excommunicating Coroticus, n 1).

Roberts, Bernadette, *The Path to No-Self*, State University of New York Press, Albany, N.Y. 1991
Bernadette Roberts is an American mother of four boys, who has always recognised herself as having a contemplative vocation, and has lived it in a very determined way. In this book she catches as few others have the challenge, the difficulty and the sheer exhilaration of spiritual living.

Roman, Jose-Maria, *S.Vincenzo de' Paoli*, Jaca, Milan 1986
An English translation of this powerful biography is in preparation. It shows the attractiveness and strength of character of another of history's great integrators.

Senior, D, and Stuhlmueller, C, *The Biblical Foundations for Mission*, SCM, London 1983
For all its scholarship this is a readable book. It shows how God's self-revelation made use of elements of Egyptian, Caananite, Hebrew and Greek culture, and it shows the 'boundary-breaking' character of Jesus himself. 'The biblical heritage,' say the authors, 'does spur us to give more weight to pastoral intuitions of solidarity with those beyond our boundaries' (p 347).

Stella, Pietro, *Don Bosco, Life and Work*, trs John Drury, Don Bosco Publications, New Rochelle, N.Y. 1985
This well-documented biography traces the development of John Bosco from an impoverished but lively schoolboy to a leading member of the 'new class of priests' who were united in the common effort to promote popular education, and to work among the sick and the imprisoned (p 106). It also describes the development of the Salesian school and the Salesian society.

Teilhard de Chardin, Pierre, *Le Milieu Divin, An Essay on the Interior Life*, trs J.B.Wall and others, Collins, London 1960
This short work has been one of the most influential in the second half of this century, mainly because of its emphasis on God's universality and immanence.

Thérèse of Lisieux, *Story of a Soul*, trs J. Clarke, Institute of Carmelite Studies, Washington DC, 1976 (1975)
Although the world has changed almost beyond recognition in the hundred years since Thérèse Martin died, her capacity to be

fully herself for those around her, and her dependence on God for that, make her autobiography still compelling reading.

Thomas Aquinas, *Summa Theologiae*, vol 1-61, ed T. Gilby, with translation and commentary, Blackfriars with Erye & Spottiswode, London 1964-1980

The middle part of St Thomas's three part work deals with what it is to be a human being and a Christian. When the work is studied from this central part out, the claim that it is the most powerful theological synthesis yet produced can be well appreciated. Although many of its details are dated, its broad lines and a surprising number of its psychological details are still valid today.

Vanier, Jean, *Man and Woman He Made Them* , DLT, London 1992

Vanier, who is a celibate, has written this book from the perspective of handicapped people, and it responds to some recent 'permissive' trends regarding their sexual lives. It expresses with tenderness and directness the issues and the potential of sexuality.

Vanier, Jean, *Community and Growth*, (revised edition) DLT, London 1989

This book describes how the most rejected people in society can give back to society what it most needs, the power to love. It grew out of the experience of living in community with handicapped people, but it has a good deal to offer to all groups.

Index